Praise for *A Widow's W*

"*A Widow's Walk* is a captivating, heartfelt story of betrayal and resilience. Burman brings the reader along on her journey from wealthy wife to grieving single parent. She finds the strength and compassion to remain devoted to her daughters, and she learns to take comfort in life's humble gifts."
—Suzanne Griffin

"A beautifully written and painfully honest memoir of how life can take twists and turns that are impossible to predict. … I commend the author for her bravery and generosity in sharing personal, painful details so that others may learn from her experience."
—Megan Rutt

"What happened to the author's family is not an isolated incident, but it is rare to hear such a well-detailed account from a wife's perspective. This very powerful read left me feeling hopeful and surprisingly not depressed. I understood and sympathized with the decisions Burman made in an effort to keep her life and family together. In this moment of attention on women's issues and empowerment, as well as the addiction crisis in our country, *A Widow's Walk* is a book everyone should read."
—Tommy Rosen, Author, *Recovery 2.0*

"It is often hard to understand the depths of emotion and hardship a spouse or partner goes through when confronted with the horrifying reality of deception. The author has been honest and frank as she helps us see her perspective and understand her struggle to move forward."
—Pam Burman

"This personal, emotional book is a page-turner, filled with insights on the challenges in marriage, friendship, family, work, and parenthood. I have been reading passages to friends, and it's sparked great, thoughtful conversations."
—Stephanie Andelman

"Written in the bold, revelatory style of Glennon Doyle Melton's *Love Warrior*, Burman reveals great vulnerability and insight. Her willingness to question who she has been as a wife and partner, and how her desires got in the way of seeing what she didn't want to see has stayed with me and inspired me to look within."
—Deborah Mitchell

"A raw, honest, heartbreaking (on so many levels), courageous, and beautiful memoir!"
—Schuy Nunn

"In *A Widow's Walk*, the author reveals parts of herself that she never thought she'd have to face, much less that would become so public. Her story landed in the scrutiny of the public eye, and not from her doing. For me, the read was brave, raw, and honest. Beautifully written and compelling, I soaked up every word."
—Merle Tabor Stern

"This book is unbelievable. I couldn't put it down. I am so inspired by the author's authenticity, resiliency, and strength. It's a must-read!"
—Jillian Copeland

A Widow's Walk

A Widow's Walk

Life Before and After My
Husband Went to Prison

JENNIFER BURMAN

A Widow's Walk: Life Before and After My Husband Went to Prison

Red Press
Wyndmoor, PA

First Print Edition, February 2018
First Kindle Edition, November 2017

ISBN: 9781977067180

Cover Photo by George Riethof / Nantucket Aerial
Cover Design and Interior Layout by Hynek Palatin
Editing by Stacey Stern https://staceystern.com/

Author's Note

I have tried to recreate events, locales, and conversations from my memories of them. In order to maintain their anonymity in some instances, I have changed the names of individuals and places. I also may have changed some identifying characteristics and details such as physical properties, occupations, and places of residence.

The author, publisher, and editorial and design teams shall have neither liability nor responsibility to any person or entity with respect to any loss or damage caused or alleged to be caused directly or indirectly by the information in this book. The author has strived to make the content as accurate as possible, but there may be errors, omissions, and inaccuracies.

I dedicate this book to every woman who has lived her life in a cloak of security and an illusion of dreams. It is for all the good girls who grew up longing for the white picket fence and the happily ever after. Those who reached for the stars and soared to the moon, then fell hard. My hope is that, in these pages, you find comfort and solidarity.

Blessing: For a New Beginning

In out-of-the-way places of the heart,
Where your thoughts never think to wander,
This beginning has been quietly forming,
Waiting until you were ready to emerge.

For a long time it has watched your desire,
Feeling the emptiness inside you,
Noticing how you willed yourself on,
Still unable to leave what you have outgrown.

It watched you play with the seduction of safety
And the gray promises that sameness whispered,
Heard the waves of turmoil rise and relent,
Wondered would you always live like this?

Then the delight, when your courage kindled,
And out you stepped onto new ground,
Your eyes young again with energy and dream,
A path of plentitude opening before you.

Though your destination is not yet clear,
You can trust the promise of this opening;
Unfurl yourself into the grace of beginning,
That is at one with your life's desire.

Awaken your spirit to adventure;
Hold nothing back, learn to find ease in risk.
Soon you will be home in a new rhythm,
For your soul senses the world that awaits you.

– John O'Donohue

Contents

Acknowledgments

I started writing this book during my husband's six-week trial. I scribbled in the little orange journal I brought into the courtroom each day, and I wrote on my phone in bed each night. It kept me sane. It kept me breathing. It opened me up and made room for authenticity.

Thank you to my sister Kim Wolfberg for reading my early drafts, for encouraging my writing, and for giving me the confidence to continue. Thank you to my sister Courtenay Wallach for being the big sister and taking care of the family in ways I never could. Thank you to my college roommate and dear friend Amy Sabel for your love and support and for asking all the right questions.

An abundance of gratitude to my editor, my mentor, and my childhood friend Stacey Stern for believing in me and for taking on my project in its infancy. Stacey, you turned my dream into a reality, and I am forever grateful.

Thank you to my yoga teachers. Each one of you has influenced me more than you will ever know. You have taught me how to be a better person.

Thank you to my two babies, Eliza and Ava. I love you both to the moon and back. Your energy and beauty, your drive and compassion, and your unconditional love and support have guided me through one of the darkest periods of my life. I have learned from your curiosity and am filled up with your laughter. Your friendship with each other and your willingness to share your hearts and dreams with me is a gift. You both are the best girls in the world.

I could not have made it through these past several years without my friends. You have been supportive beyond words. Thank you for loving me just the way I am—shit show and all.

A huge thank you to my family. These past few years have been hard on everyone. We all have been grieving. While it has not always been easy for me to accept and receive the love you send my way, I appreciate it more than you know.

Thank you to my mother and father for your patience and faith as I have figured out my next steps. I am blessed to have loving parents who support and guide me. Mom, you are giving and strong. Dad, you are truly the most incredible man I know. You are the glue that holds us all together. I love you both.

Thank you to each and every person who has helped me transition into single parenthood. Helping care for my girls, listening to me, and offering perspective. You have sent me books, fed me, taken care of Dasher, helped me move, weeded my garden, given me gifts, practiced yoga in my studio, and loved me and my girls. You have been by our side. You are too many to name, but you have carried me. I am grateful and blessed to be surrounded by your love.

Every single one of you contributes to my life and makes me a better person. I am only able to shine with the guidance of your light. I love you all.

CHAPTER ONE

Convicted

Whenever my mind would wander to consider hypothetical ways my husband might leave me, "going to prison" never made the list. Heart attack, motorcycle accident, cancer, or infidelity. Those were the usual suspects of my ruminations. While I tried to manage my anxiety, I contemplated the possibility of Matt's death and my subsequent abandonment far more often than I'd like to admit.

Being with Matt for nearly twenty-five years fostered a profound dependency. I couldn't imagine life without him. This fear led to a smoldering obsession that somehow, someway Matt would leave me. And leave me he did. Little by little at first; then ultimately, in a rather unconventional manner.

My story, my marriage, and my circumstances are not what any woman hopes for. Even in my wildest fantasies, I never could have imagined this tale would be mine to tell.

I had everything I thought I needed and wanted in life. I was married to my soul mate, my knight in shining armor. Matt had charmed me from the start. He was honest, kind, open, and confident. He was exactly who I was seeking in a long-term partner, and he was the antithesis of what I was used to. He rescued me from a long history of relationships with the wrong kinds of boys.

We met in Telluride, Colorado, in 1991 when we were both in our early twenties, and we fell fast and hard for one another. I was attracted to his chiseled jaw, full head of longish hair, incredible smile, and clear blue eyes. At 5'9", he was broad-shouldered and 175 pounds of perfect athletic proportions. His direct gaze and immediate warmth caught my attention and held it for twenty-five years.

We spent our first year together falling in love and learning about one another. After traveling and enjoying an alternative, adventurous lifestyle in the beginning, we gradually made our way to Philadelphia, where we'd remain for the next twenty-three years. It was my graduate school education and the promise of career opportunities that lured us back East. Optimistic and brilliantly in love with each other and life, we were ready to take on the challenges and adventures that awaited.

We got married along the way, and my husband became a highly successful businessman. By 2014, we were in our forties, and had been married for eighteen years, with nine- and eleven-year-old daughters. We were blessed by loving families and friends. And we owned two beautiful homes, including our dream beach house on Nantucket Island, Massachusetts.

I was living the dream I thought I wanted. But there were cracks in the veneer, and everything was about to be laid bare—on February 19, 2014, to be exact. That is the day my husband, Matthew Edward McManus, was convicted by a jury of conspiracy to commit three counts of money laundering, two counts of wire fraud, and one count of mail and wire fraud. He was also convicted of obstruction of justice and making false statements to the federal government for his involvement in an advance fee fraud scheme with five coconspirators who all plead guilty.

According to the judge and jury, Matt, Arlen Greenberg (Matt's partner and co-owner of New Reality Capital), and their employees collectively defrauded 1,946 people out of $26 million. They did so by offering to connect borrowers seeking loans for commercial real estate projects with money providers, and requiring the borrowers to pay non-refundable advance fees.

Apparently (and I reflexively insert "apparently" because at the time I absolutely could not or would not believe Matt knowingly, willingly engaged in this), Matt's company failed to secure, or even attempt to secure, financing for the vast majority of borrowers who paid advance fees for their services.

It took the jury a mere ninety minutes to deliberate the case before returning with a guilty verdict on every charge. Even so, I believed from the bottom of my heart that my husband was innocent. I believed every word Matt uttered when he was indicted then tried then convicted, which was that he was guilty only by association. Matt assured me that while he ran the company's Philadelphia office, he had no idea that his business partner, Arlen, was orchestrating a multi-year, fraudulent scheme from the company's Chicago office.

Matt had no shortage of explanations for his unjust indictment and conviction.

"I was indicted because I'm the only one with real money, the only one who can pay retribution."

"The prosecutor has it out for me because I told him to fuck off when he asked me to help them convict Arlen."

"Because I was an initial partner in the company and have been there since the 1990s, they assume I must be part of the scheme."

"Arlen still owes me money. How can I be guilty of anything if I didn't personally make a profit?"

"All my deals were legit."

In addition to accepting at face value everything Matt said (which I admit reveals me to be avoidant, to say the least), I simply could not fathom my husband in prison. Even if I could have entertained the possibility that Matt might somehow be involved in fraudulent activities, no one could have convinced me that he deserved to be penalized with anything beyond financial retribution to the victims.

I clung not only to Matt's conviction that he was innocent of all wrongdoings but also to his insistence that he himself was a victim. He was the scapegoat. I continued to believe this even as all five of his alleged coconspirators pled guilty. In fact, it seemed more plausible *because* they pled guilty while Matt was willing to fight the charges and defend himself to the bitter end.

The art of denial is powerful. While I trusted my husband wholeheartedly, I also wanted everything to be all right. I wanted this episode to blow over so we could continue living our lives in the ways we had become accustomed. More than that, I did not want to lose Matt. I did not want our family to be broken.

Matt lawyered up when he was indicted, and I stood by his side. Emotionally and physically, but not intellectually. I chose to ask certain questions, but not all. I failed to educate myself on the details of his case. I was overwhelmed, overly trusting, and underprepared. Frankly, I just couldn't deal, so I resorted to my usual coping skill. I put on my game face and prayed for the best. If I hadn't chosen to use denial and ignorance as my protective shields, I would have been forced to reevaluate the increasingly passive role I had assumed in our marriage.

Throughout the months of seemingly endless meetings with Matt's lawyer, then growing team of lawyers, I chose to accompany Matt to only two such meetings. Perhaps most significantly, I chose to disregard the advice we received from two bold, dear friends who urged, "Settle with the government. Do not go to trial!" My brother-in-law Adam said to me one day, "The government does not like to lose."

I listened only to Matt's continual reassurances and blocked out the rest. From the day he was indicted two years prior to his conviction, then all the way through his sentencing, which occurred nineteen months later, Matt and I were united by the goals of keeping him out of prison and our family intact. We were in survival mode.

With that mindset (and I beg for your non-judgment), I didn't much consider the victims who allegedly suffered at the hands of Matt's company. I didn't want to believe Matt had anything to do with it, and I chose to tune out many sordid details. My questions were self-serving and basic, such as when I'd ask Matt for the hundredth time, "What do you think the chances are, in terms of a percentage, that you will end up in prison?" He would always tell me zero. I believed him, and that would calm my fears, at least for the moment.

But the trial was excruciating. It was painful for obvious reasons like having to hold my head high each day while I felt the jurors' scrutinizing eyes upon me. And for feeling vulnerable and shattered while trying not to cry or shout out and interject when I knew certain statements to be false. At times, I wanted to stand up and scream profanities at the prosecutor and Special Agent Kelley, who I blamed for putting us in this courtroom.

I felt powerless, small, and bereft. I would glance at my father sitting next to me and feel a mix of embarrassment and appreciation. I was ashamed my husband put our family in this horrific situation, and I was simultaneously awed by my father's undying support. My father was impeccably dressed as always, and he also was extremely nervous. He had a hard time sitting still, constantly shifting his position on the uncomfortable, hard bench. When I looked over at Matt's parents sitting on the other side of my father, I ached as I witnessed his father looking supportive and guarded and his mother looking pained and steady while she knit a very long red scarf. When I tried to put myself in their shoes, I hurt as only a parent could.

I was shocked and horrified to hear the charges directed at Matt and the details of the accusations coming to life through the prosecutor's verbose, painstaking illustrations. It wasn't until the trial that I became aware of the longevity and severity of New Realty Capital's scandalous activities. It sickened me to hear how things had been meticulously orchestrated and taken to such an extreme level, causing suffering and hardship for so many people.

I became convinced that Matt didn't stand a chance, whether or not he was actually guilty. In the months leading up to the trial, Matt repeatedly told me the prosecutor was lazy, "an idiot," and his case would be sloppy and weak. Sitting in that courtroom proved otherwise.

Seated behind Matt in the courtroom, there were days I had to stifle my tears as I watched his head lower and his broad shoulders slump in defeat. I had put Matt on a pedestal of strength and invincibility for so long. It was painful to see him show signs of weakness. Yet somehow his vulnerability brought much-needed doses of reality and humility to the surreal courtroom environment.

Even so, I longed for Matt to continue to be the rock he always had been. To hold me up and prevent us from drowning. But this rock was made of sand, and it was crumbling.

The day Matt's trial ended with his conviction, I started writing in earnest and haven't stopped. I don't know how I would have weathered the past few years without the safe haven of my journal. I dumped my anger, fears, and confusion onto its pages as I tried to process the mess my life had become.

Initially I wrote with shame. When I started exploring my questions about whether Matt might actually bc guilty, it felt like I was betraying him. As his wife, I believed it was my duty to stand by him no matter what, and that applied even to loyalty in the furthest recesses of my mind. I was terrified to examine what might hurt our marriage and to confront the skeletons we both had been hiding.

Yet I had to understand what happened to my husband, to me, and to our once healthy, caring relationship. I started at the beginning when we first met and oozed love, compatibility, and promise. Then I revisited my childhood, the universal launching pad through which many of our values take shape.

As I wended my way to the present, I struggled to look for clues. Not only about who my husband was and what led to his conviction, but who was I? Who did I used to be? What had I lost along the way? What did I want back? Who were we as a couple, and who are we now?

I tormented myself with questions like, "What did I miss?" "If I paid more attention to Matt's business or his legal troubles, could I have done something differently?" "Could *we* have made better, different choices as a couple—and if we had, would Matt be in prison today?"

Sometimes I wish I still could believe he did nothing wrong, that he would never put himself or his family in harm's way. But money is a great seductress. Initially, we both enjoyed the excess; our pleasure was mutual. Then it seemed that Matt couldn't get enough. His hunger for the next deal and the next check was insatiable.

The more he got, the more he craved. The very thing that alleviated his pain of college debt and brought him the safety and security he hungered for, was also what destroyed him. An endless quest to everywhere and nowhere all at once. He had eagerly jumped into a lucrative business that was thrilling at first but became toxic along the way.

Money. Power. Delusion. Losing oneself. Or, in my case, allowing myself to get lost then attempting to find myself again. All this and more bubbled to the surface as I struggled to process my experiences and unearth old memories.

My writing was unstructured and cathartic. Although I approached it as if I were writing in a diary or journal, I knew I wanted to turn my rambling work into a book.

In fact, for as long as I can remember, I have wanted to write a book. I just didn't know what to write about until my life was turned upside down. While I wouldn't have wished for this material, it is what has been bestowed upon me.

I wrote to grieve, reflect, learn, and try to heal. I never wrote with a desire to hurt anyone. And I sincerely hope I haven't. To protect the privacy of others, I have changed the names of many of the people as well as that of my husband's company.

The past several years of my life have shaken me loose from a slumber of stagnation, apathy, and indifference. I am waking up to a reality that feels painful and alive. My memoir grew from a place of basic human need. Organic and open, writing became my salvation.

Pouring my feelings into my journal then transforming it into a memoir has served me in ways that were previously unimaginable. Writing has become part of my therapy, joy, motivation, focus, breath, and soul.

This book is an excruciatingly raw and honest attempt to reduce to words the transformation that has occurred and continues to unfold within and around me. It is about love and heartbreak, trust and marriage. It is about delving deeper into self-discovery than I previously thought possible and facing head-on the pain and conflict that emerged. It is about loneliness and dependency. It is about self-reliance and expectation. It is about loss and renewal.

One of my greatest personal challenges and faults has been my tendency to not see my goals through to completion. I am in constant fear of putting myself out there and being rejected. This book (besides raising my girls on my own) has been my first huge leap of faith, and the first time I've pushed myself, trusted myself, and loved myself enough to see it through.

CHAPTER TWO

Legal Nightmare

Spring 2012

The legal nightmare that culminated with Matt's conviction thrust itself into our home on Friday, May 4, 2012. It was just before Shabbat, the one night of the week Matt would come home from work in time for us to have dinner as a family. There was a chicken in the oven. I was relaxing on the green velvet sofa in the family room, looking out the picture windows and noticing new growth on the trees as our daughters played outside.

I was enjoying a peaceful moment when the phone rang. It was my friend Iris.

"Oh my gosh, Jenn, I am so sorry to hear about Matt. What can I do for you?"

"What are you talking about?"

It was at that moment from my dear friend, who happened to have read a Google feed that came across her computer, that I learned of Matt's indictment.

I had less than a minute to process this when the phone rang again. It was Matt.

"Hi. ... Jenny I have something important I need to tell you." His voice sounded reluctant and vulnerable. It was unusual for my husband to sound frightened. There are very few things in life that rattle his cage. "I was indicted today, just now."

"What does that mean?" I was calm at first, just listening. I can't recall much of what he said during that call. I was too busy being stunned, I suppose. While I had known this was a possibility, it seemed utterly unlikely.

Four years earlier, an article in *The Wall Street Journal* asserted that New Realty Capital had engaged in fraudulent practices. That article came out just before Matt's fortieth birthday, as we were preparing a special celebration, and Matt assured me at the time that there was nothing to worry about. Matt said that the firm's problematic behavior was confined to the company's Chicago office and specifically tied to the company's founder, Arlen Greenberg.

Matt's confidence that Arlen's problems wouldn't become our problems dispelled any concerns I may have had. I clearly did not understand the implications. Nor, to be frank, did I try to understand. Matt told me what I wanted to hear, and I barely gave it another thought.

Looking back now on that celebratory fortieth birthday weekend in Nantucket, I recall happily welcoming friends and family to the island and to our home. I was buzzing with the excitement of having everyone together. Speeches were being prepared and cakes were baking as I coordinated last-minute details for a spectacular Fourth of July celebration under a blue-and-white-starred tent on the beach at The Galley restaurant.

The intimate group of twenty family and friends came to our house to kick off the celebration with cocktails on the balcony. It had been a gorgeous day, and the sun was still hot but starting to dip. It was that perfect time of day at the beach when all feels right with the world. Matt, his brother, and two of our dear friends were sipping martinis and talking quietly. As I walked out on the deck to join them, the mood seemed serious, not at all befitting the vibe I expected. In my characteristic avoidance of all things unpleasant, and to make sure I kept the energy exciting and positive for the celebration, I minimized this overtly tense moment. It is obvious to me now that they were talking about the salacious article and possible consequences.

Another distinct recollection from that weekend occasionally resurfaces and taunts me. It was the day after the party. Although we were tired and hungover, a small group of us took Matt's boat out to Coatue, a pristine stretch of beach accessible only by boat. We were sunning and lazing on the hot sand. Jeff, who worked with Matt and was a close friend, was sitting next to me and asked, "How do you do it? How do you handle stress so well?" My reply was simple. "Yoga." It was the honest answer to what I wanted to believe was a straightforward question.

But I can no longer deny the sincerity and depth of his question. Of course he was referring to the serious legal problems and dysfunction in Matt's company. It bothers me to consider what he may have made of my flippant response. Did he think I knew what was going on? And if I did, that I would be that nonchalant about it? I am often tempted to pick up the phone and reach out to Jeff, but I am scared.

Ever since Matt's conviction—or perhaps more accurately, ever since Jeff testified against Matt in court—we haven't spoken. Jeff and I used to be very close friends. I met him in Telluride even before I met Matt, and I shared a house with him and several others when I first arrived in town. I also was extremely close with his sister, who also owned a home on Nantucket. In the end, it was Jeff who cooperated with the FBI and wore a wire to help incriminate Matt and reduce his own punishment.

Back in May 2012, when Matt told me he had just been indicted, I didn't even understand exactly what "being indicted" meant. But when I heard the fear and hesitation in Matt's wavering voice, I knew his nearly impenetrable wall of confidence had been breached.

After we hung up, I sat there in silence, running my fingers along the smooth fabric of the sofa and looking out the large windows at the beautiful spring afternoon. The sun was beaming into the room, casting a soft light that spilled onto the dark wood furniture. I was struck by the contrast of the surrounding scene.

The cherry trees that Matt and I planted years before in honor of the birth of each child were in their full glory, bursting with soft white blooms. As the wind caught hold of the petals, they fluttered carelessly to the ground. In light of the crushing news that had just been delivered, I suddenly felt anything but careless.

The arraignment occurred several days later. When I asked Matt if I should accompany him, he said it wasn't necessary. Matt later told me he was ordered to report to the courtroom, where a judge read his charges. Matt responded "not guilty" and was released without bail. While he was able to continue to travel within the US, his passport was confiscated. He also was assigned a probation officer, Angela, to whom he was ordered to meet with weekly.

Angela was kind and humble. A tiny woman with sad eyes and a south Philly accent, she came to the house several times to ensure Matt was not a flight risk. She appeared uncomfortable during these home visits, as if even though this was her job, she was self-conscious about intruding. She would come in quickly, look around the house, and ask a few questions. She always asked me, "How are you holding up, honey?" I didn't realize then that she felt sorry for me. She knew exactly what was coming and had seen my type before. The innocent, naive wife who had no idea what was about to hit her.

The final condition of Matt's arrest was that he not speak with any "potential witnesses." This was extremely challenging since one of them was his brother and another was his assistant Jackie. Following his court appearance, Matt and his attorney went to the US Marshals office, which Matt described as "a windowless, cement-floored room, with jail cells down the hall." Matt was fingerprinted and mug shots were taken before he was released. He referred to this process as "the longest hour of my life."

Matt was trying to shelter me from the harsh reality that was unfolding, but I can't help but wonder: If I had gone with him to witness firsthand and get a sense for myself how very serious this indictment was, might I and might we have made different, wiser decisions moving forward? We will never know.

CHAPTER THREE

In the Beginning

Autumn 1991

I know my husband well. Or at least I thought I did. We met when we were both twenty-two-year-old college grads living in Telluride, Colorado. It was an easy start to what quickly became a serious relationship. We met in October 1991 in a cozy bar called The House, a bright blue restored Victorian perched on top of Oak Street in the heart of town. I remember staring at Matt from across the bar. My friend David noticed and said, "He has a girlfriend." The next thing I knew, Matt walked over to me and introduced himself. I was immediately smitten.

We talked for hours that night. He was present, straightforward, and humble while also being confident and smart. His thick, chestnut brown hair was a little long, but he was not the hippie type I tended to date. Matt was a preppy New Englander wearing khakis, a button-down oxford, and a black fleece vest. I was attracted to him right away. His chiseled jaw had an adorable cleft, and his sparkling blue eyes with impossibly long eyelashes never left my face while we talked.

He seemed devoid of the ego and immaturity I typically experienced with guys my age. I don't remember what we said to one another when the night ended, but I know we didn't exchange phone numbers. There was no need. In a town as small as Telluride, it was a given that our paths would cross again soon.

The very next day as I was leaving the public library, I ran into Matt as he walked out of the Floradora Saloon, the restaurant where he worked. He asked if I wanted help carrying my books up to my house, which was a steep walk, also on the top of Oak Street. I said yes and we walked together and talked. He left me at the door with my ridiculous pile of books. The books found a resting spot at the foot of my futon bed, where they remained untouched.

A couple of nights later, I was out with my new group of friends at The Country Club, which despite its name, was a dive typically crowded with locals looking to fill their bellies with the all-you-can-eat offerings. Drinks were cheap, the music was loud, and it was Friday night. Everyone was looking for a good time.

My friend Jill and I had arrived in Telluride just a few weeks earlier by way of a cross-country drive from Nantucket. We were following our dream of carefree living in a quaint ski town and temporarily staying with a friend of a friend. Rent was pricey in this up-and-coming resort town, so when we first arrived we were lucky to have been offered a spot on the floor of the bedroom David shared with his roommate.

It took us two weeks to find our own place. We moved from David's bedroom floor and into a wonderful little house down the street from theirs. I felt damn lucky that we were able to rent this cozy, newly built carriage house, with its large loft bedroom and sunny French doors that looked out to Bridal Veil Falls in Telluride's famed boxed canyon.

I was also grateful that Jill and I were so warmly welcomed into this East Coast come West group of Dartmouth, Swarthmore, and Yale graduates. That night at The Country Club felt full of promise. As I made my way to the salad bar, there Matt was again. I was excited to see him. Balancing our plates in one hand and our drinks in the other, we walked over to the bar. I told him about my upcoming road trip with Jill. We were planning to go to Aspen to see the Spin Doctors. He asked if he could join us. I asked about his girlfriend.

I had since learned from David that Matt moved to Telluride with his girlfriend from college, who David described as sweet, petite, and blond. Matt told me he was not in love with her anymore and planned to break up with her the next day. His revelation excited and confused me. He knew he wanted me, and although I didn't know what I wanted, his bold move swept me off my feet.

Even so, I engaged in my usual over-thinking and panicked a bit. Matt seemed so right for me, but I had come to Telluride single after yet another yearlong relationship had ended, and I was looking forward to seeing what it would be like to casually date. I was a relationship junkie with a history of rushing prematurely into serious, monogamous partnerships—intense relationships that typically would last a year or so before ending abruptly and painfully.

I was trying to make changes, and I had mixed feelings about Matt pursuing me so intently. I wasn't ready to make a commitment or put my heart on the line so soon after the disasters I experienced with my past several boyfriends. Or, in fact, with all my love affairs. Crazy, messy love interests that always left me in a heap of self-loathing and apathy until I found another guy to whom I could tether my heart.

While I was uncomfortable with Matt's decision to break up with his girlfriend, I was simultaneously intoxicated by his act of impulsivity. "Are you sure this is what you want to do? Um … do you really want to end it with her because of me?"

He was unusually open and communicative. He assured me he had no expectations. He gratifyingly told me that he was very attracted to me, and that it would be unfair of him to remain with his college girlfriend given his feelings for me.

Matt was not discouraged by my hesitancy. The next day I found a rose and a card on my pillow. I still have the card. There is a picture of a sunset on the front, and on the back he wrote, "I couldn't wait to get down the mountain so I could bring you this note. I have to admit that it was hard to keep my mind on my skiing. Love, Matt"

That is how our relationship began, and while it was fast and furious, it also was gentle and easy. I was nervous to open my heart to him, but there was no game playing. He made it safe and easy to love him. Matt knew what he wanted and was confident in a way that refreshed and exhilarated me. We spent almost a year together in Telluride.

Our time there was largely carefree, and our relationship was uncomplicated and organic. After dating for just six months, I moved out of the little house on Oak Street and into what was known around town as The Red House. It was a barn on an old homestead a mile out of town.

Matt had been sharing this sweet place with three fraternity brothers. When I moved in, they moved out, and Matt and I had the old house to ourselves. It was rustic and charming, and I couldn't have been happier. This was the first time Matt or I had lived with a romantic partner. He was hesitant about taking that step, but for me it was a no-brainer. I couldn't wait to live together. I was certain this was the right move for us.

Summer in Telluride has a completely different vibe than winter. Brilliantly sunny days in the San Juan Mountains are complemented by dark, cool nights. The Bluegrass Festival is an annual highlight, with thousands of earthy, music-loving folk populating the sleepy town, pitching tents along the creek and in the valley, partying in the festival campgrounds from sun up till sun down.

That summer's festival is well preserved in my memory. I wore round, blue, Revo glasses with my short, patchwork, hand-stitched hippie dress. My thick red hair was as long as it has ever been and Matt's hair was also long. I had asked him grow it out, and although that's not really his style, he indulged me. We listened to Emmylou Harris and James Taylor as the hot sun warmed me inside and out. I felt young and lucky. I was in love with Matt and in love with life.

On our days off from work, we'd hike up Bear Creek and Telluride Falls. We naturally fell into a rhythm of domestication while getting to know one another more intimately. I worked at a Native American jewelry store called Hell Bent Leather and Silver, which I loved. Matt worked long, hard, ten-hour days building houses. It was a coveted, lucrative job, but also one that took up most of his time and energy. He often came home from work worn to the bone. After a beer and pasta, he'd head straight to bed. While our relationship wasn't always as romantic as I may have liked, I was thrilled to finally have my first serious boyfriend with whom I consistently felt comfortable and nurtured.

After a continuous string of serious relationships that I had beginning at the age of fourteen, my relationship with Matt was the first one in which I felt safe enough to be my true self. I could let my "crazy" show ... my emotional ups and downs, insecurities, anxieties, faults, anger, and my tendency to test my partner to see if he would love me or leave me. Matt saw all my good, bad, and ugly, and he didn't falter.

I tested limits plenty in prior relationships. My fears about not being loved and accepted for who I truly was, with all my dents and imperfections, often left me less than confident. I would push boyfriends away to see what would happen. Would they love me? Leave me? Push back? I wanted proof that no matter how badly I behaved or how flawed I was, I was still worthy of their love. Matt was the first person in my life who loved me how I wanted and needed to be loved.

My relationship skills were both seasoned and damaged. I was addicted to being in a relationship and didn't feel whole without one. Feeling empty without love, I spent time with guys who weren't good for me, over and over, short-term and long-term. With so many failed relationships, I didn't know how to do "easy." While I hungered for it, I needed to be taught how to love and how to trust. Matt did this for me and with me. He was a kind, gentle soul with whom I decided to surrender my guard. After just a few short months together, I knew I would marry him.

Even so, those Telluride summer nights sometimes left me lonely and wanting more. Always more. More attention. More love. More filling the emptiness deep inside me. My expectations in relationships had never been realistic. I was raised in a strongly couple-centered home. My parents always made it clear to me and my sisters that their union and their relationship came first. They did not allow their daughters to take center stage or otherwise take precedence over them.

The house I grew up in often felt loud and chaotic to me. My mom was a yeller, and I was extremely sensitive. I often sought refuge from her frequent fights with my older sister, Courtenay. To cope with familial discord, I fantasized about a quiet, peaceful home where everyone got along and nurtured one another. My mom told me that all families were like ours, and I wasn't going to find The Brady Bunch in anyone's home.

My mom and dad never let the challenges of parenting interfere with their bond, their marriage, or their life. My father was king and my mother was queen, and they took excellent care of each other. While I admired their genuine commitment to loving and doting on one another, as their child, I sometimes felt there was not enough left for me.

Of course my parents loved me. But I was a textbook middle child who hated controversy. And I was emotional. Never wanting to be the source of trouble, I would quietly retreat to my room and aloneness. My attempted goal was avoiding family drama and chaos. My achieved goal was isolation and longing.

While the value of being in a relationship was impressed upon me throughout my childhood, I received mixed messages. My young, hip parents were supportive of me having long-term, increasingly intimate relationships. Beginning in eighth grade, I had serious boyfriends. I was always "in love" and always permitted to go on dates, where I would be dropped off at the movies or driven to a boyfriend's house to hang out, whether his parents were there or not.

Michael was my first true love. He was sweet and smart and a caretaker. My parents loved him. He reminds me of my husband's best qualities. But after my relationship with Michael, I learned about sex and its power. I was emotionally and hormonally driven for the next decade. Misguided and misunderstood, my teen years were the beginning of identity and self-esteem issues that I still struggle with today.

I was boy crazy and looking for love in all the wrong places. My parents' actions and words were not always parallel. While they encouraged the serious boyfriend thing, my mom also used to say, "You need to have choices. You need to keep your options open." All I know is that from a very young age, much of the love I yearned for felt like it came from boys. I had such an urgent need to be paired that when I was briefly "single" at age fifteen I felt hollow.

When Matt entered my life, I finally began to relax. I was eager to let my guard down. My search was over. I felt lucky, satisfied, and relieved to have found my partner. Someone who wasn't a "bad boy." Someone who would not break my heart. Someone I could trust. I could now focus on my lifelong mate and start planning my fairy-tale version of our future. Where we would live, the jobs and careers we would have, who our friends would be, what hobbies we would share, how our families would embrace us … my fantasies and expectations were unbounded.

My mother has told me that, as a child, my outwardly non-needy, low maintenance nature was a welcome respite for her. She was just nineteen years old when she gave birth to Courtenay, and twenty-one when she had me. By the time my Mom was twenty-five, she had a six-year-old who had challenged her from the start, a four-year-old, and an infant. I can't fathom being that young with so much responsibility.

While Matt and I experienced a different kind of relationship in our early twenties than my parents did at our age, making ends meet was a central focus of ours. One of the reasons Matt worked so hard that first summer in Telluride was so he could afford our upcoming travel adventures. I didn't yet know what it meant to work hard to support myself financially. I had always been extremely well provided for. My parents had paid for private high school and my college education. I didn't have any school loans. When I graduated from college, my parents continued to pay for my car insurance and health insurance. I paid for my remaining expenses—rent, food, and entertainment. Easy.

In stark contrast to my very comfortable upbringing, Matt began working hard when he was eight years old. His first job was a paper route that he worked 365 days a year.

He kept this job throughout much of his childhood. He then moved on to bussing tables in restaurants and later took care of people's boats. By the time he was sixteen, Matt was buying himself many of the "extras" he desired, such as Levi's jeans, ski equipment, and junk food, such as Pop-Tarts and Little Debbie snacks. There was no money for these treats in the grocery store envelope his father would leave for his mother on the kitchen table as cash allowance for the provisions of a household of four boys and several dogs and cats.

In my childhood home, there was a junk food drawer filled with Pop-Tarts, Entenmann's cookies, Tastykakes, and Hostess treats. My closet was perpetually crowded with designer jeans and cowboy boots. My purple velvet Gloria Vanderbilts were my favorite in sixth grade. By age thirteen, I was handed a credit card four times a year (as the seasons changed), sent to Bloomingdales at the White Flint Mall, alone or with a friend, and given a very generous amount to spend on my wardrobe. I remember feeling overindulged, yet also elated. I was stoked to be able to buy pretty much whatever I wanted. It was during these formative years that my values around money began to take shape. Looking back, I see how my ambiguity, double standards, and love-hate relationship with money played a significant role in my habits of spending and saving.

By the time Matt and I were living in Telluride, I had gift money from my Bat Mitzvah and college graduation sitting in a savings account, and he had nothing, actually less than nothing. He was responsible for financing part of his college education and was thousands of dollars in debt. I recall getting my first phone calls from debt collectors in The Red House. Matt had started his adult life like many other college graduates—full of promise and chained to debt.

It was not until much later that I saw his desire for money grow exponentially. Truth be told, in the beginning his motivation for financial success was highly attractive to me. I saw him as goal-oriented and driven to succeed. I loved that he wanted to be a provider. I interpreted this as his loving me and taking care of me. On the one-month anniversary of our first date, he bought me a beautiful silver Hopi bracelet with waves etched into it. He presented it to me in a tiny box with a red ribbon at La Marmot, a rustic French restaurant. We had champagne with dinner. I loved his attraction to nice things and his desire to please me. I felt cherished.

Matt spent his childhood in the wealthy New England towns of Andover, Massachusetts, and Essex, Connecticut. Early in our courtship, he'd talk about how he always felt financially inferior to his peers and his surroundings. He was jealous of the kids who had Levi's jeans, while he had to wear Toughskins. He coveted his neighbors' houses where the paint wasn't peeling. He envied his friends whose families owned the boats that he worked on. One of Matt's childhood wounds stemmed from his material insecurity and self-imposed pressure to keep up with the Joneses.

I was proud of his self-made character and admired his intelligence and drive. I would not have predicted that his desire—or more accurately, our shared desire—for the American Dream would destroy us.

CHAPTER FOUR

Wanderlust

Summer 1992

Traveling has always been one of my greatest joys. Once Matt earned enough money at his construction job, we planned our first adventure together. It was the summer of 1992. With our AAA TripTik in hand and my cherry red 1988 Saab 900s packed with tents, blankets, clothes, Windsurfers, and provisions, we began a three-week journey that turned out to be the trip of a lifetime.

Our first stop was New Mexico, where we fell in love with the magic of Taos and Santa Fe. We hung out with a college roommate of Matt's, Thea. She took us to a magical authentic Mexican restaurant in the center of a beautiful outdoor courtyard, where the margaritas were made with fresh lime juice, and the tequila was as pure as the agave plant it came from. They tasted like sunshine. We went hiking and found a cow skull on a dirt road, which I later painted and which became a decorative item in our homes. We camped in the pouring rain and stayed completely dry in our pup tent. We scoured the art markets for local paintings and fell in love with the desert light. We soaked in the famous pools at Ten Thousand Waves and ate huevos rancheros every morning. Next we camped our way through the National Parks and Canyons in Utah, staying at several KOAs (Campgrounds of America). Moab and Salt Lake City were our two main stops before we entered Idaho. There we stayed at a sweet campground by a small lake. From Idaho we drove over 400 miles to reach Matt's heaven on earth, Hood River, Oregon.

Friends hosted us for nearly a week. I have pictures of our blue tent pitched in their side yard. Next to the tent loomed a huge Oregon white oak with an old-fashioned rope swing and wooden slat bench seat. In one photo, I am swinging high and laughing. I remember when the picture was taken. It was one of the happiest moments in my life.

Windsurfing the Columbia River Gorge was a dream come true for Matt. While he windsurfed, I spent much of the time huddled in my sleeping bag attempting to avoid the whipping sand and praying Matt wouldn't get killed. For him, the sport was only exciting if the wind was blowing hard enough to make it almost unbearable for those on shore. I wasn't surprised to learn that spectator girlfriends like me were referred to as "windsurfing widows." I certainly couldn't have foreseen that I'd face a different kind of widowhood later. But during that vacation, Matt was as happy as I had ever seen him, and I was impressed by his fearlessness and his skill. I was drawn to his adventurous nature and, back then, also his risk-taking tendencies.

Seattle was our next stop, then down through sleepy towns along the Washington and Oregon coasts. I much preferred the quiet beauty of the small towns over the cosmopolitan feel of Seattle. But it all felt good—romantic, exciting, full of possibility.

I will never forget the Great Sand Dunes in Oregon. We each rented a dune buggy. I was clueless about the topography and how to control the vehicle on the steep sand hills. Several times I found myself completely vertical at a dead stop because I didn't get enough speed to make the climb. I thought I was going to die. I screamed as loudly as I could. Blinded by the white sand dunes, I sat there in complete fear until Matt came to my rescue. Twice.

We also visited Portland State, one of the three graduate schools to which I had been accepted. I liked it a lot. I thought it was a good choice for my graduate education, and I hoped Matt would consider Portland a nice place to land for a couple of years.

From there, California was a blur of one beautifully dreamy beach town after the next— the Bay Area, Monterey, Carmel, Santa Cruz, and Big Sur. We then hit the desert roads and headed inland to the Sierra Nevadas. In Lake Tahoe we splurged on our first motel. It was seedy and awful. It was raining hard as we both squeezed into a phone booth to call home on Mother's Day. That was the end of our trip, and we drove a long way on desert roads back to Telluride. We shared the planning of this trip equally, hitting some of the spots that each of us wanted to. We traveled well together. Matt did all the driving. He knew I preferred being the passenger. For the next twenty-five years, whenever we were in a car together, he drove. I loved him for taking this burden from me.

Traveling with Matt felt natural and comfortable. It seemed like a good omen for a positive future together. Although we were on vacation with only minor decisions to make, I enjoyed the ease of our chemistry. I had been on short camping trips with past boyfriends that hadn't fared nearly as well. My journey with Matt was idyllic, exciting, bonding, and validating. We were deeply in love, and our dynamic was like nothing I had ever experienced.

We were both hooked on adventure. By the end of the summer we decided to move to Maui. Before he had moved to Telluride, Matt lived with friends for three months in Kauai, windsurfing every day. He wanted that again. Hawaii was Matt's dream, and I was up for the chance to continue our athletic, alternative lifestyle. I put off graduate school for another year in the names of wanderlust and love.

Most of the money we saved that summer went toward our $800 plane tickets. After leaving many of our belongings and my Saab with my friend Alec in Boulder, we were off to the Aloha State.

When we landed in Maui, I felt far from home. I was unsettled and unsure. We stayed with one of Matt's friends in Kihei for a few days while we looked for a car and a home. We found a rental home high in the hills in a rural town named Haiku. It was northwest of Paia and fairly remote. We also purchased a junker car for $600—a 1980 light blue station wagon perpetually on the brink of collapse. It was October, and the heat was oppressive. I remember looking at the massive pile of shoes that I frivolously brought with me. I shoved them into the back of my tiny closet and didn't touch them again for the next eight months.

Although our tiny bungalow didn't have air-conditioning, it did feature an open-air shower frequented by huge banana spiders. Our bed was a futon mattress on the floor. While it was comfortable, I often had trouble sleeping after seeing the hugest, hairiest Hawaiian centipede scurry across the room inches from my face. Did I mention they are poisonous?

The best feature of our place easily was the deck from which we could see the Pacific Ocean several miles in the distance. I was not entirely happy in my new home, but I knew Matt was excited to be on this island of wind and water. I supported his dream and soaked in all that Maui had to offer.

We both got jobs at an Italian restaurant called Casanova, located in the small, hippie town of Makawao, high up near the volcano. I was making good money serving cocktails to tourists and surfers while Matt served dinner in the main dining room. His career as a waiter didn't last long. He got fired because he didn't memorize the extensive menu and repeatedly delivered the wrong orders to customers.

I was disappointed he didn't try harder and furious he let this perfect job opportunity slip away. As irrational as it may have been, I thought if Matt loved me enough he would have done what was needed to keep the job we picked as a team. Even if that meant studying the names of each entrée and corresponding ordering codes on the computer. My expectations were high. I wanted a responsible partner and a provider. He was broke, so I made him collect food stamps until he found another job. We joked about this later, but at the time, I am sure he felt awful.

My disenchantment lingered even though Matt immediately found two other jobs—one at a windsurfing shop and one bussing tables at the well-known restaurant, The Hali'imaile General Store. The long commute to our respective jobs and our constant car troubles and car sharing made our time on Maui strained.

On our days off, we explored the island, which was wild and rustic and beautiful. But I was homesick for Colorado. Maui was the antithesis of Telluride, where I felt completely at home and at peace. Here, I didn't surf and didn't fully relate to the culture. It was hard to make ends meet, our car was unreliable, and I was miserably hot all the time. But Matt wanted to surf, and I wanted him to be happy. When we left in April, I was ready.

After Hawaii, we ended our free-spirited lifestyle and slowly made our way back East. First, we stopped in Colorado to pick up my car and visit with friends. I had deferred my entry to grad school long enough and knew it was time to get to work. Matt, too, knew it was time to begin a career that would help him pay off his school loans and begin saving for the future we wanted with each other.

CHAPTER FIVE

East Coast Reality

Summer 1993

Matt and I moved to Philadelphia in the summer of 1993 so I could begin a two-year graduate program in social work at the University of Pennsylvania. My undergraduate degree from CU-Boulder had been in psychology, and I had always been fascinated by interpersonal relationships and family dynamics.

My parents were big believers in the power of therapy. I attended many strange but intriguing family therapy sessions as a child, which I didn't particularly enjoy. I remember not talking when the psychologists asked me questions.

By the age of fifteen, I had moved homes and switched schools several times. I was acting out and depressed. The therapist I was sent to left a lasting but this time positive impression. She used to knit while I would tell her my problems. Her eyes were always on mine. I never understood how she didn't have to look down at the sweater she was working on.

I have always been drawn to helping but also to analyzing, for better or for worse. I want to understand why people behave in the ways they do. My favorite movie and book in sixth grade was *Sybil*, about a woman with dissociative personality disorder. It was scary and shocking and so messed up. To this day my infatuation with mental illness is almost voyeuristic. Not only was I fascinated by Sybil's multiple personalities, but I also was confused about my own family dynamics. I fell into the mediator role—maybe I put myself there or maybe it was a natural fit—but nonetheless my career path seemed to be forged from a young age.

While I wasn't thrilled about two more years of school, I figured it was better than the five it would take if I opted to get a PhD in Psychology. I had several jobs in the mental health profession when I was an undergraduate. Teaching art in a community mental health center and teaching cooking skills to residents in a halfway house not only gave me credits toward my degree, but also gave me experience that undoubtedly helped me get in to the University of Pennsylvania.

Philadelphia was a stark contrast in every way to the natural beauty and lifestyles we had experienced in Colorado and Hawaii. To me, Philly was a depressing, huge, harsh, dirty city. Our first year living in town on 19th and Callowhill was a low point in my life. Thank God I had Matt and school to keep me busy. I hated living an urban life. The grime, the homeless man Bill who lived outside my building, and the ice storms that winter were oppressive and made me feel claustrophobic.

But for the first time in my life, I was focused on doing well in school. I loved my classes and was a good student. The plan was to graduate in two years, leave Philadelphia, and go back out West to live and work as a family therapist.

When I started at Penn, Matt got a job selling alarm and security systems for a company called Vector Home Security. A natural salesman and self-starter, he excelled at his job. I was proud and impressed with his work ethic. He spent most evenings driving around the suburbs, knocking on doors, or on the phone making cold calls. He also sold Herbalife products on the side. Matt was always looking for the next opportunity, so when one of his coworkers mentioned a job opening in the real estate industry, Matt jumped on it. Here began the ill-fated relationship with Arlen Greenberg and his company, New Realty Capital.

Matt approached this opportunity as an all-you-can-eat buffet. He excitedly described Arlen as a self-made success, and a soft-spoken, confident, humble family man.

"A brilliant businessman," I recall Matt saying. Arlen was a devoted father to his sons from his first marriage as well as to his new wife and young son. Arlen was in his early fifties, and Matt and I looked up to and adored him, his wife, and their children.

Not once did I question why this man was taking a risk in bringing Matt in to his fold. I am extremely trusting and generally believe people have the best of intentions. I am learning late in life that sadly this is not always the case. Hidden agendas, looking out for Number One, lying, and cheating. Moral values fallen by the wayside. Duplicity. As I look back on this innocent and thrilling time in our young lives, I can't help but feel venomous toward Arlen Greenberg.

When Arlen invited Matt to join New Realty Capital in the spring of 1994, Matt readily accepted. The job involved sales, which Matt loved, and learning about the real estate world, which had always seemed exciting to him. The hours were flexible, and he would be learning from a man he admired.

Thus a mere eight months after we moved to Philadelphia, Matt had begun his career in real estate. Arlen was the commander-in-chief and Matt was his willing warrior, ready to do battle and win in a competitive industry. Over the next twenty years, Arlen would be many things to Matt—mentor, business partner, friend, foe. But back in

1994 there was not a moment's hesitation nor any foretelling that Arlen and his relationship with my husband would lead to the toxic nightmare that would tear our lives apart.

In fact, things were great for a long time. Matt was immediately successful in the real estate lending and mortgage business. He was a born dealmaker, and with Arlen's established business relationships and guidance, Matt began earning a lot of money quickly. Within just one year, Arlen invited Matt to be his partner in the business.

Matt derived tremendous satisfaction from his increasing income and corresponding professional achievements. In turn, I was incredibly proud of his hard work, and I loved the lifestyle that his growing income afforded us. A travel junkie, it was exhilarating to plan amazing weekend getaways and luxury vacations. I became quite spoiled.

Matt had a hard time saying no to me. He enjoyed traveling and nice hotels as much as I did, but it was he alone who took on the stress of paying for these extravagances. I never for a moment worried about money. It wasn't how I was wired. Karma is now taking hold of me by force.

Matt used to call me entitled. When he used that word, I listened. His description was accurate. I assumed Matt would always be a success. That he would take care of the investments, carry the burden of our bills, and wisely manage our money—just like my father did for my mom and our family.

Since Matt liked all things finance and was calm under pressure, I was in denial about how much stress he endured. He rarely expressed concern although he talked about money constantly. How much he was making was usually the focus. He was seeking praise and validation. From time to time, he would show me bills and request that I decrease my spending. I now see that he was attempting to rationalize, categorize, and organize our spending to dilute his anxiety. He sent me mixed messages, and I heard only what I wanted to hear.

I wish he more explicitly communicated his concerns to me. Maybe he tried. I wish I had been a better listener. Matt also was a lavish spender. I rationalized, "If Matt is making as much money as he continues to brag about and spends thousands of dollars on fancy watches, fine dining, and a $25,000 stereo system, I can buy Chanel purses and hand-stitched Belgian curtains at $150 a yard." We were both out of control.

But at the time, I thought I was happy. I was unable to recognize the dysfunction, and I felt lucky to live a lifestyle that we enjoyed so well and at such a young age. We had just purchased our first house in Glenside, Pennsylvania. A three-bedroom brick 1950s colonial with a new kitchen and a pretty garden, and my life at the moment felt complete. During those early years in Philadelphia, Matt and I had a very close bond. We were best friends. It was rare for us to spend time apart. I was very attached to him and found it difficult to share him with friends and family. I was sinking deep into my dependency of Matt as my partner, friend, lover, and most destructively, my provider.

After I graduated from Penn with my MSW in the summer of 1995, my father was turning fifty, and he and my mother treated their three daughters and significant others to a family vacation in Aspen to celebrate his milestone birthday. Matt and I had been living together for three years by then and had talked a bit, but not too much, about getting married. It was becoming the elephant in the room, but we both wanted the progression to be romantic, so we opted to talk little about the inevitable next step.

After our family time in Aspen, Matt and I drove to Telluride. On our second day there we went four-wheeling in the mountains and discovered a spectacular spot by a stream, with wildflowers surrounding us and the San Juan Mountains seemingly an arm's length away. It looked like we were literally on top of the world.

We laid out a blanket and the provisions we brought from Rosie's Market. Matt took a small bottle of Champagne out of his backpack, got down on one knee, and asked me to marry him. Time seemed to stop. When I screamed, "YES!" he pulled a black ring box out of his pocket. I was thrilled. I loved Matt very much and knew he was the right man for me.

He placed the ring on my finger. It was a stunning 1.5 carrot solitaire flanked by two baguettes, set in a simple platinum setting. It was perfect. We spent the rest of the day exploring the mountains until we blissfully made our way back to town where we told everyone we saw—all strangers—we had just gotten engaged.

When we got back to our hotel room at the Ice House, we called our parents to share our happy news. Then we capped off our day with dinner at Campagna, one of our favorite restaurants. I have beautiful photographs of the spot where we got engaged, which I memorialized by painting a picture that hangs on the wall above the fireplace in our "Colorado Room," which is what we call our family room. The feelings I had on this day felt strange, happy, and somehow rehearsed. Like a movie that I had been playing in my head for twenty-five years.

Newly engaged and with my graduate degree in hand, I began my career as a family therapist. I immediately joined a private practice just ten minutes from our home. My work was extremely challenging, and while I sometimes was in a bit over my head, I was proud I took such an autonomous and advanced job right out of school.

Most of my grad school friends said they were too intimidated to go into private practice right away.

The issues my clients presented were varied, and included chronic depression, panic disorders, anxiety, marital discord, sexual abuse, ADHD, addiction, and chronic pain. It was a lot for me to handle at times, but my fake it till you make it attitude got me through the early months, as did my determination to establish myself as a reputable therapist in the community.

CHAPTER SIX

Marriage and Children

Summer 1996

Matt and I got married on Nantucket Island in June 1996 in a fairy-tale destination wedding. By then Arlen and his wife were among our closest friends. They, along with dear friends of my parents, were staying at The Wauwinet, a secluded resort on Nantucket Bay. When I walked out to the breathtaking beach where they had arranged chairs in a semicircle to visit with one another, I was overwhelmed with joy that these very special people had all gathered to celebrate with us. I still find it hard to reconcile how I felt on my wedding weekend with what we are going through now. When I look back in my mind's eye at that day on the beach, I am heartbroken.

After our wedding, Matt's income grew steadily. It was a no-brainer to trade in my Saab for a BMW and to shop at Ralph Lauren instead of Banana Republic. I felt especially validated by my parents when they complimented me on a new designer outfit. I comfortably transitioned from being a full-time to a part-time therapist. I loved our luxury vacations to Nantucket, St. Bart's, and New Zealand. I was proud of Matt for paying off his student loans. When he purchased his first sports car, a previously owned 1990 black Porsche, I was happy for him. A little less so when he would race it on a track in New Jersey, but I knew this was part and parcel of the daring and exciting man I married.

I relished our Saturday date nights. We both loved to dine out, and I enjoyed keeping up with the growing Philadelphia restaurant scene. I was proud of our home and spent time decorating it and learning how to garden. Matt enjoyed participating in these hobbies as well.

We also loved throwing parties. Our annual holiday soiree was always fancy and fun. Our friends would come down from New York and Boston just to attend. I tried my hardest to replicate the pages of the then-popular *Martha Stewart Living* magazine. I would make elaborate vodka drinks with flowers frozen inside of ice cubes and decorative towers made from lemons and limes. It was generally a carefree time in our lives.

We had been married for five years when we decided to transition from coupledom to parenthood. But when we started trying to conceive at age thirty-five, it took us a year. At the time, this felt like an eternity and placed a lot of stress on our marriage. I blamed Matt for his slow-swimming sperm due to his pot smoking. We sought help from a fertility specialist. After a few months of temperature taking and several doses of Clomid, we were pregnant. Our relief and excitement erased our challenging year, and we were on a new journey.

The next nine months were happily filled with doctors' appointments, sonograms, baby names, birthing classes, and nursery decorating. In the midst of all of that, we decided to buy a new house! I was bursting with baby and with joy.

At 11:30 p.m. on November 11, 2002, we became parents with the arrival of Eliza Jane. Named after the Radiator's rendition of *Little Liza Jane,* but legally named Elizabeth after Matt's maternal grandmother. Our little girl entered our lives with a shock of black hair and her eyes wide open. I immediately sensed her unique nature. We were drenched in bliss and unaware just how radically our lives would soon change.

We were very grateful that the pregnancy was uncomplicated, the birth was easy, and our daughter was healthy and strong. We were ecstatic and surprised that she was a girl because we were convinced I was carrying a boy. My entire family, including my sisters and their husbands, my parents, and even Fay and George, my parent's longtime housekeepers, were in the waiting room. I was overjoyed with love for my newborn and by the support of my family.

It didn't take long for me to discover, however, that parenthood would significantly challenge my partnership with my husband. Eliza was born during one of the coldest, snowiest winters on record in Philadelphia. Having an infant kept me inside the house for most of that bitter winter. I was often overwhelmed and isolated, and I became increasingly depressed.

Our jet-setting lifestyle a distant memory, I was consumed with keeping this tiny foreign creature alive and well. I was scared to death. We were fortunate to have a baby nurse for the first few weeks. She showed us how to care for our daughter, as I was anything but a natural. I didn't know how to change a diaper, let alone how to figure out what Eliza needed when she cried for hours on end. I cried when the baby nurse left. Feelings of fear and isolation lodged further into my psyche.

Waking up every few hours to feed Eliza spawned a nasty relationship with insomnia. The sleeplessness was so persistent that I'd occasionally hallucinate. I was so anxious about her well-being and survival that I couldn't relax. I also was struggling with my own attachment issues from childhood and so desperately wanted to be the perfect parent that I was making myself crazy.

Yet while I was wandering through the fog of severely sleep-deprived motherhood, Matt's life seemed relatively unchanged. He continued his workaholic ways, typically coming home after Eliza was in bed. He was often out of town, regularly traveling to New York, Florida, or Las Vegas to build partnerships and close deals. I both respected and resented his hard work. I experienced a confusing emotional push-and-pull that I largely kept to myself. When I tried to share my mixed feelings with Matt, he became defensive. I learned to hide my feelings and found some solace in being passive-aggressive, which of course only ignited the flames.

When Matt wasn't working, he liked to play golf and work in the yard or wax his cars and smoke cigars in his garage. He also liked to crunch numbers. I know he tried hard to balance his new role as a father with his work, hobbies, and attentiveness to me, but our relationship suffered immensely. We were rarely intimate, and when we did have time alone, I often felt distant and numb.

We each felt highly neglected by the other. Our needs may have been different, but the result was the same. We both felt disconnected and wounded. I was still in the grip of my fantasies of perfection. I wanted us to be just as great at parenthood as we used to be as a couple. When we fell short, I became increasingly anxious and angry.

According to my perfectionist ideals of great parenting, Matt didn't measure up. I thought he would offer to do the baby's middle-of-the-night feeding. I thought he would hear her cries and get up so I could sleep. I thought he would stop drinking and smoking so he'd be more capable of handling the baby. I thought he would share my worries and obsessions about feedings (on-demand or scheduled?), napping (once or twice a day?), and bedtime (let her cry it out or rock her to sleep?). I felt abandoned by what I perceived as Matt's lack of involvement, and he felt overly criticized by what he perceived as my not thinking he was doing a good job at whatever tasks he did. He was right. I *was* critical of his caretaking. We were not a pretty picture.

I didn't live up to my own ideals either. I had an image of myself as a relaxed yet doting mother. I wasn't comfortable in my new role. Nothing about mothering felt calm or easy for me. I envied the mom who casually breastfed her child while chatting with other mothers at the park. I wanted to be the mommy who spoke soothingly to her crying infant. Or the mom who could carry on an intelligent conversation without obsessing over her toddler's needs.

If Eliza was hungry or fussy while we were out, I'd suddenly want to rush home to tend to her there. Panic would set in. Many days I didn't manage to get out of the house at all. Loading the stroller into the car while making sure I had packed every item that the baby might possibly need always seemed to turn into a frenzied and time-consuming shit show. Everything felt like a mountain. Everything felt strained and pressured.

My initial disappointment with Matt's lack of parental involvement morphed into resentment. Matt made it clear that his role in our partnership was to make the money and pay the bills, and my job was to handle everything else. While I didn't mind handling our social and domestic matters when it was just the two of us, now Matt's insistence on a clear division of labor hurt. Before I became a mom, I was able to handle him turning down my requests for help in the kitchen or social planning. But now I needed him more. I felt like I was parenting on my own. It was lonely. Our prior decade of closeness and intimacy receded as our day-to-day lives rapidly diverged.

When Eliza turned one, I was shocked to discover I was pregnant again. I had barely begun to feel comfortable as a parent and couldn't imagine how I'd manage two. Yet we were deeply blessed on December 23, 2004, with the birth of Ava Frances. We named her after my maternal grandmother Freda Frances White, "Nana," who had passed away just months prior and with whom I had a very special and close relationship.

Ava was a sweet, easy baby, but I found it challenging to juggle a two-year-old and an infant. True to my self-defeating nature, I turned to self-loathing. Other moms seem to manage just fine, what is wrong with me? Why aren't I more capable? Why can't I manage two babies, look beautiful, have a sparkling house, and keep a smile on my face?

Much to my chagrin, we hired a part-time nanny from Trinidad, Hazel. I hated that I needed her, and I felt horrible that I was apparently incapable of taking care of my girls and my home on my own. I, who so disliked having nannies growing up, now relied on one. I once told my sister, "I will never have someone else help me raise my children." The inaccuracy of my prior declaration taunted me.

When the girls were babies, my days were all the same. It was mind numbing and exhausting. I tried to feel enthusiastic about how many ounces of milk Ava drank or what kind of new berry Eliza tried. Highlights of my week consisted of putting on jeans and makeup for the pediatrician and making it to my mommy and me class on time. Social outlets were few and far between, and my life as an individual adult woman seemed to come to a standstill.

In my pre-parent days, I thought Matt and I would seamlessly incorporate our baby or babies into our lives. I dreamed we would bring them along to our Saturday night dinners. I thought endlessly about happily toting them along to our weekend errands and carrying them in Baby Bjorns on our hikes in Valley Green.

Even though many pictures in the photo albums that now sit in neat, colorful piles beg to differ, I remember a constant undercurrent of angst, panic, and tension. I tried too hard to make everything perfect. I wanted to be completely hands on. And I wanted it to be fun. And I wanted it to be a shared partnership.

Reality proved no match for my fantasy. I was hypervigilant about my children's needs. Consequently, I could not enjoy myself in any social situation that included my children. I envied the parents who could let their kids crawl around the kitchen floor while they seemed relaxed, cocktail in hand.

Although I was deeply conflicted about hiring Hazel, having a nanny allowed me to go back to work a few days a week, get out of the house, and enjoy quiet Saturday night dinners out with Matt. While I relied on Hazel for the much-needed reprieve, it was not without emotional fallout.

Matt was proud he could afford a nanny. I begrudged him for using her presence to justify his absence. Having a nanny allowed Matt the freedom to nurture his workaholism. Or quite possibly the freedom to avoid my discontent. He would often come home just in time to say good night to the girls, drive Hazel to the train station, and hang out with me for an hour before going over to his home office/man cave to work until 1 or 2 a.m. He'd then be too tired in the morning to get up with me and the girls. On weekends he would not wake until after the girls and I were well into our day.

Meanwhile, I felt like a failure each time I'd hand the girls over to Hazel and walk (or sometimes sneak) out the door. I was anxious when I was not home. Sometimes Hazel was at the house and I'd be too tired to go out, so I'd stay home. I felt so uncomfortable, having a visitor in my home who was caring for my children seemingly better than I. Even though Hazel worked for us for many years, I never made my peace with the arrangement.

Disabused of the notion that Matt and I would take a modern approach to an equitable sharing of domestic duties and child-rearing, our marriage became staunchly traditional in terms of gender roles. It would remain that way until Matt went to prison.

CHAPTER SEVEN

Post-Indictment Life

Spring 2012

Matt was indicted on April 26, 2012. Our girls were seven and nine. The news broke in the *Philadelphia Inquirer*, and an article in our local *Springfield Township Gazette* appeared a week or so later. When I initially read the articles, I was in denial. Matt told me the accusations were lies, and that the people portrayed as victims were opportunists trying to take advantage of New Realty Capital.

My emotions were tightly wrapped in a confused bundle. At first I was highly protective of Matt. Later came shame. Had I really married someone who could be accused of such hideous crimes? I was furious with Matt for letting something so awful seep into our otherwise beautiful lives. I felt naive and stupid for not seeing this coming. Yet I also trusted what my husband told me about the accusations. I didn't believe them to be true, and how dare anyone say these harsh things about Matt?

Now, several years later as I write this book, I continue to resist my editor's inquiries about my feelings about the victims. I am not ready to go there. I don't have it in me to open one more fissure in my cracked, shattered landscape. To open the floodgates of feelings toward hundreds of families might just kill me.

I am broken, but I am not the only one. I ache for my girls, my husband, Matt's parents, and my parents. I am pained for my and Matt's siblings for the brother they lost, and for my sisters for the sister they lost, as I am not the same person. I hurt for Matt's close friends, especially Mark and Gunti. Maybe someday I will be able to let in the pain of the hundreds of victims affected by my husband's actions. For now, I don't know where to put it.

In the immediate aftermath of Matt's indictment, I was in survival mode. I turned to Matt as my sole source of information, and attempted to refute the allegations leveled against him. This was challenging, especially considering I didn't even know the exact definition of "indict." I had to look it up in the dictionary to see it meant "1. A formal charge or accusation of a serious crime. 2. A thing that serves to illustrate that a system or situation is bad and deserves to be condemned."

Initially I fielded phone calls from friends and neighbors who learned of the indictment on their own accord; either from being in the real estate business or from reading the newspaper. I was hypersensitive about Matt's indictment and the publicity surrounding it. I'd fluctuate between nervously blurting out the truth to anyone who asked me how I was doing, to pretending that life was perfectly fine.

Then there were our families. Mine was very worried and rightfully so. I spoke to my sisters and parents, answering their questions and concerns as best I could. I didn't have enough information to offer my family or friends who reached out. They wanted to know details and asked me dozens of questions I couldn't begin to answer.

I could not wrap my own head around the situation. Fearing judgment, I was highly guarded. The calls, e-mails, and texts were emotionally draining. I found myself trying to explain and justify Matt's actions. At the time, I truly believed he had been wrongly accused.

Matt's Catholic parents are stoic by nature. His father is Irish Catholic and his mother is of Italian and Belgian descent. Conversations with them about the indictment were relatively straightforward, with zero drama or hysteria. They spoke mostly about the specifics of Matt's legal case and how to keep him out of prison. His loving, caring parents seemed quite able to keep their emotions in check.

I can't even imagine their pain in facing the possibility that their firstborn might spend a very long time in prison.

After the initial chaos of the indictment receded, our lives returned to "normal" on the surface. For the sake of Eliza and Ava, and determined not to lose the next year to worry and depression, we forged ahead. Matt changed. He was softer, humbled, and vulnerable. He and I became closer than we had been in years.

Matt was spending fewer hours at the office. In the face of losing everything, he came back home to us. Many surmised that Matt's pipeline of business would come to a halt—that the Philadelphia real estate community would distance themselves from him. Friends and family frequently asked me, "Do people want to continue their business relationship with a man who had been indicted for seven criminal acts?" Apparently they did. In fact, no one seemed to give a fuck.

Nonetheless, given his impending trial, Matt tried to keep as low a profile as possible. He contained his public self and limited his networking. He kept his head down and worked hard and modestly. As long as Matt continued to secure funding, the deals kept coming in.

By day, Matt continued to close the complicated, high-risk deals he was known for. On nights and weekends, he prioritized the girls and me like never before. Witnessing Matt in a vulnerable place, perhaps for the first time ever, made me fall in love with him again. He needed me. And I needed him to take care of me, of us, and to make everything okay.

Some were surprised that Matt's indictment didn't up-end our relationship. To the contrary, while the year between his indictment and conviction was emotionally charged and challenging, Matt and I were becoming more loving with each other. We both felt appreciated in ways that had been buried and nearly forgotten. Our crisis brought us back to each other. I didn't know how we'd ultimately weather the continual losses, but to feel connected again was simultaneously heartbreaking and beautiful.

***

Spring 2014

In the spring of 2014, the trial was over, and I knew my husband was going to prison. I was regularly overcome with an anger that was ugly, bitter, hostile, and forceful. The intensity of my emotions and their expression confused me. I would typically direct my verbal lashings toward my husband, parents, or siblings, trying desperately to spare my children. Right after an outburst, I would become overwhelmingly melancholy. This ensuing sadness made me feel raw and vulnerable in ways I never had before. In the past, I rarely cried. But that spring my tears were prolific, a seemingly endless river of sorrow. It felt oddly good. Sadness being the pure form of what is usually more easily accessed as anger. Crying felt cathartic and productive.

The heightened state of my emotions during that period still feels alive to me. Even now, it's difficult for me to reflect on that time without feeling like I am caught up in it again. Perhaps that's why I'm now drawn to shift into the present tense as I continue sharing my story.

So, here we are in the bizarre period between Matt's conviction and sentencing. We know he'll be going to prison but we don't know when, where, or for how long. The clock is ticking, and our time together as a family is soon coming to an end. Might it feel something like this when your doctor says, "You have a few months to live"?

Time feels precious, every minute significant. When I find myself in a situation that I don't want to be in, even for a few hours, I get annoyed and angry. I want to control everything. Since I can't, I vacillate between anxiousness, anger, and depression. I try to live in the moment, be present, and hold onto tiny pockets of joy. While this has always been difficult for me, the effort feels heavier now, as if every move I make is more urgent and significant. A blanket of pressure hovers over me.

Yet there still are moments when I am grateful for the earth beneath my feet and the roof over my head. Grateful for my health and my capabilities, my family and friends, and simply for being alive. As clichéd as this may sound, I believe in karma and the yin and yang of life. I understand I must endure pain to fully experience pleasure, and that one does not exist without the other. I believe that everything happens for a reason. While I don't think Matt or our family deserves this fate, I sense that somehow, somewhere we will learn of its greater purpose. I just wish I had the foresight to know it now.

Yesterday I was on a conference call with our team of lawyers, which has grown to the financially daunting number of three. The agenda was to place a dollar figure on the collective financial loss to the victims—a number we might actually be able to pay back during our lifetime. Currently, the victims' losses are estimated to be $29 million.

What I had hoped would be a productive call, seemed more like a dance between corruption and capitalism set to the tune of bureaucratic protocol. I had to hang up before the call was over because I was at the girls' school and they were about to get into the car. At this point, the legal fight does not seem worth the minuscule stirrings of hope that occasionally penetrate my otherwise bleak reality. I am fairly certain what the future holds. I know Matt is going to prison for a long time. Does that mean three years or ten years or more? I don't know. All I do know is at the end of this year, Matt will be taken away from us.

I think about all the things he will miss. Ava's tenth birthday. Eliza's first middle school dance. Christmas. The girls' Bat Mitzvahs. Family vacations. Sadly, the girls will miss as much if not more. The rough and tumble play with their father, his help with their Apple devices, Sunday night outings to CVS and Starbucks, the laughter as they play games with our dog, Dasher. My head spins.

I don't know what I'll do when my best friend and partner of twenty-three years is no longer here. Lying with him in bed at night after the girls fall asleep, talking or reading, just being. The void on his side of the bed. I panic at the prospect of having to take care of the children's every need without his help. Even with him here, I am often overwhelmed and exhausted. Each evening I am grateful when Matt walks through the door. I expect weekends will be especially tough. I am up at 6:30 a.m. every morning and now that the girls are growing up, they are pushing for an increasingly later bedtime. They are typically awake until 9:30 p.m., while I am completely spent by 7:30 p.m.

While both of our families have generously offered to help, none of them live nearby. The one who lives the closest is my younger sister Kim, who lives with her husband and two children in New York City.

Matt has helped me a lot in recent months. He has become a true parenting partner. Who will I now turn to when I need to drive Eliza to dance class and need to take Ava to a party at the same time? Who will help with algebra homework? Who will fix the dishwasher or the printer, which regularly malfunctions? Who will tickle Ava's back for the fourth time because she is having a hard time falling asleep while I am in Eliza's room helping to ease her science test anxiety?

I contemplate numerous scenarios for the future. Perhaps an able bodied, rent-paying person will move into our guesthouse. Preferably someone with superior math skills, who is technologically savvy, a lover of Pomeranians, a fearless bee killer, and strong snow shoveler. Or maybe we'll move. If Matt gets placed in a facility in Oregon or Texas, we'd have to follow him, right? I have wanted to get the hell out of Philadelphia since the day we moved here. These fantasies, however, serve little purpose other than to placate my nerves momentarily. In just a few short months, I will be in the same single parenting, husband incarcerated predicament no matter where I am or who lives in our guesthouse.

I obsess over the impact Matt's absence will have on our girls, and I am terrified I will feel lost without him.

There will be a huge void in our family unit. Matt is the great equalizer. He rounds me out, softens my seriousness, and adds comic relief to an otherwise ritually laden day. The girls adore him. There is always laughter when he is around. I am strict, often moody, and sometimes I can be mean.

My doctor thinks I need a low dose of an anti-depressant. I will take it. I want to be a kind parent. I want to be tolerant and nurturing. Yelling and losing my patience while I help Eliza with math or I brush the ever-present snags out of Ava's hair does not make me feel like a good parent. I want my children to experience me as present, reliable, and consistent. So I take the twenty milligrams of Prozac daily. It quells my anger a bit.

In February when the trial had become unbearable, I asked for something to help with my anxiety as well. I was prescribed Ativan. Sometimes it helps, yet I know it's just a crutch. I occasionally take it to stay calm or when I feel the effects of my morning yoga wear off. It feels like protection. Shielding me from me. I worry about becoming dependent on the Ativan. When I share this concern with my friend Cari, she reminds me that I do not have an addictive personality. It's a relief to hear her say it.

I fantasize about becoming an avid drinker. Perhaps two glasses of wine religiously each night. I briefly wonder if this would make me a nicer person. But I know I'll never do it. For starters, I hate wine. And beer. Drinking is not my go-to for stress relief. I enjoy a drink socially when it's celebratory and in an ideal setting like at a party, out to dinner with friends, or lying on the beach in Mexico. The idea of pouring myself a drink as I hurriedly prepare tacos to feed the girls before we rush out for their thrice weekly, three-hour gymnastics practice sounds impossible and unappealing. Self-soothing with substances is not my thing. Unless we consider sugar a substance. Which I'm pretty sure it is these days. In that case, I probably should detox immediately.

My saving grace besides my yoga practice is the unconditional, objective, give-and-take that only a professional therapist can provide. I see Nancy every other week. She is tremendously helpful. Petite and grey-haired, she is maternal, intellectual, and spot on. I always feel clearer and lighter when I leave a session. I usually cry a little, and letting go feels like a relief, a necessity. The ease of truth that flows while I am in her office is deeply healing.

Lately we have been traveling back together into my childhood. I'm well aware I carry around an unhealthy amount of anger from my past. I sometimes cling to the wounds I experienced as the middle child in a family where, at least from my perspective, there was a lot of emotional drama and verbal volatility. I was highly sensitive, and the perpetual screaming was scary and loud. I took refuge in my bedroom with its Kelly green shag carpet and bright floral wallpaper that covered the entire room including the ceiling. Safe in my twin bed, with the door shut tight, I would escape into my books.

My favorite was *The-All-of-a-Kind Family* series. The stories, which are set in the early 1900s in Brooklyn, New York, revolve around five Jewish sisters in a close-knit, poor, immigrant family. The girls were best friends and shared many adventures while being solidly led by their parents. The warmth that poured from these books felt like a blanket. My mother told me families like the ones portrayed in my novels didn't exist, but this didn't stop me from dreaming.

While I am deeply grateful that most of my friends, family, and neighbors have been incredibly supportive in the aftermath of Matt's conviction, the exceptions are notable. Like the couple in Chestnut Hill who have been our good friends for over twelve years and now want nothing to do with us. She helped me decorate my home. He shared business with Matt. We have been to each other's homes, enjoyed many nights out on the town together, and celebrated milestones together. A fiftieth birthday party for her. A fortieth birthday party for me. Now when they see us walking down Germantown Avenue they turn the other direction. It has happened twice. I shouldn't be surprised, but I am. It is hard not to feel a knife in my heart when I am the recipient of this kind of insensitivity.

My friend Maureen asked me if this was painful. "A little at first," was my response. The art of denial coming to my emotional rescue. This couple exemplifies the superficial, insular nature of some Chestnut Hill natives. They tend to exclude those who don't fit the homegrown preppy mold that can only be acquired by living in this blue blood town for generations. I guess their concern about social appearances took precedence over kindness and empathy. Fragile relationships become transparent when challenged by discomfort. Yes, I was hurt. Yes, it was painful.

In contrast, I feel blessed by the supportive nature of my many true friends. They have shown up for me in the most loving and generous ways. They have taken me out for lunch and sent cards, e-mails, and texts just to check in. They keep calling me even when I don't return their calls. In some cases, they've offered the use of their second homes or even money. They have taken care of Dasher and provided countless rides home for the girls. One friend helped with the exorbitant private school tuition. They have given the girls babysitting jobs and other odd jobs to help with pocket money. They have given me career ideas. They have not judged me, and they have been supportive of my path, even when I stray.

My family offers the same—even more. Yet my childhood wounds run deep, and I'm finding it hard to be around my parents, my sisters, and my in-laws right now. Being with them feels pressured and complicated. It brings me too painfully close to the reality of my looming future without Matt. Everyone feels sorry for me, and I hate being the source of pity. This feeling of being untethered has left me stumbling in a wake of uncomfortable shame.

I love my family and know they want what is best for me. I understand that they, too, are suffering. My mother and father are pained not only as parents but also as grandparents. Both of them have gone to extraordinary lengths to be there for us. They even put their own lives on hold and moved to Philadelphia for Matt's six-week trial.

While my father sat next to me in court every day, my mother seamlessly took over my household responsibilities. She drove out to the house each morning, walked Dasher, went to the grocery store, prepared dinner, picked the girls up from school, and shuttled them to their various activities.

The girls were thrilled to have their grandmother Gaga fill in for me. In fact, Ava and Eliza weren't even aware then that their father was on trial. We told them Gaga was in town to take care of them while I helped Daddy at work because his assistant was sick and would be out for a while.

That quelled any curiosity they may have had as to why I was suddenly leaving the house each morning dressed up for several weeks in a row.

When I'd return home from the trial each evening, I'd be worn to the bone and deeply grateful that my mom was there. Despite my parents' incredible support, I continue to be hard on them as I struggle to shed old hurts and find healthy new ways to interact.

I just finished writing my letter to Judge Anthony. We are trying to collect 300 letters. The purpose of these letters is to provide the judge with insight into Matt as a person, father, and friend. At this point, I don't have a lot of faith in the process or that this will actually help reduce Matt's sentence, but we'll find out soon enough. I imagine these letters can't hurt. Every other one makes me cry.

On the way to the girls' gymnastics class tonight, seemingly out of the blue, Ava asks about Matt's placement. She is curious and concerned about the distance of the facility and its accommodations. "Will Santa be able to visit him in punishment camp?" (She refuses to call it prison.) "Will Daddy be able to leave for holidays? Will we be able to talk to him on the phone every day? Can we bring Dasher with us when we visit? Will we have to move if he is far away?"

Then Eliza, "Will I be able to postpone a Friday test until Monday if it is a visiting weekend? Can we call

Daddy two times a day, once before school and once before bed?"

These questions break my heart, but I respond as directly as possible. I have found that as with most things, the girls follow my lead, emotionally and otherwise. The conversation soon turns to their upcoming end-of-the-school-year party, which has been a tradition in our household since the girls were in pre-school. In the span of ten minutes, I field five or six questions about prison, then set the date and come up with a guest list for the girls' pool party. I am strangely proud of this small conquest.

CHAPTER EIGHT

Last Nantucket Summer

Summer 2014

Matt's sentencing is delayed sixty days plus one week, so we won't find out where or how long he will serve until the end of July. Amazingly, it looks like we'll still be able to go to Nantucket this summer. While our financial situation is seriously compromised, by some grace of God, our houses have not been taken from us through forfeiture or otherwise. At least not yet.

The girls and I are scheduled to leave for Nantucket at the end of June. Matt's probation officer grants his request to join us for the first two weeks as well as the last week. He will go home the third week to be in the office and work. We are thrilled to be given this final gift together as a family. Life at our home on Cisco Beach, Nantucket, is simple and easy. Our days there are filled with surfing, reading, boating, paddle boarding, home-cooked meals, and a trip to The Juice Bar almost every night for the best homemade blackberry ice cream in a hot waffle cone. Everything about our island home nurtures my spirit and makes me feel blessed to breathe the salt air.

We have been going to Nantucket as a family every summer since the girls were born. Matt and I rented the tiny cottage next door for six consecutive summers after we married. In 2004, the year Ava was born, we bought the house next to our humble rental. Buying a vacation home on Nantucket was always a shared but distant dream. Neither of us anticipated this reality so early on. We were over the moon. The house has become our haven, our home away from home, our pride and joy, our happy place, our dream come true.

The memories we have collected as a family on Nantucket are priceless. Our lives are much simpler there. We don't watch television, we don't have a landline or a computer, and we don't get mail. It is healthy and joyous. We shower outside and visit with neighbors on the expansive beach. Occasionally, friends or family visit. We always celebrate Matt's Fourth of July birthday with lobsters and clams at the house then a trip on the boat to see the fireworks.

While it's hard when our time on Nantucket comes to an end each summer, it will be much worse this year. This time when we leave, we will be putting the house on the market. Selling the house has been a confusing, complicated decision. There has been no shortage of advice. But the bottom line is that I am going to need money while Matt is incarcerated. The Nantucket house is in both my and Matt's name. When we sell it, I assume the government will want Matt's half right away.

We arrive in Nantucket on the official first day of summer to seventy degrees and a cloudless sky. Our house, which we call Wind Moor (a maritime play on words of Wyndmoor, the Pennsylvania town we live in), is perfect in its open, airy, simplicity. The houses on our little street are uniformly grey-shingled and trimmed in white or grey. Blue doors of about five different historical society approved colors are the norm. We are one of the lucky few who have a widow's walk, a small square deck on top of the roof from which one can see for miles. The name is said to come from the wives of mariners, who would watch for their husbands' ships to return from long journeys at sea. This was in vain when the ocean took the lives of the whalers and left the women as widows. The irony of the widow's walk is not lost on me at this fateful time.

The driveways are made of crushed clamshells, and the landscaping is clean and simple with hedges, garden gates, and hydrangeas along the perimeters of the yards. Plum roses line the split rail fences that mark the dirt roads along the beach. Wild blackberries will start to bloom in a few weeks. Cisco Beach, which draws surfers from across the island, lies just beyond our front door. We can see the ocean from our bedroom and living space. Sitting on the deck, looking out at the Atlantic is the sweetest gift.

Upon arrival, we head down the sandy path to a beach that is empty but for a few early summer surfers. Seals frolic in the blue green water. I go in up to my knees. The water is cold and refreshing. Discarded snail shells, round and perfect, are scattered along the jagged water line that marks the water break. The occasional conch or quahog shell can also be found. The air smells of beach plums and Rosa rugosas mixed with sweet new summer grass and salt water. The small waves lap quietly.

As we settle into our time on Nantucket, I find some peace, but even this peace feels different. A shadow lingers. Sometimes it slightly taunts, like a faint bruise that remains tender. Other times I see my future hovering over me like a cartoon bubble that antagonizes: "Don't get too comfortable. Don't be too happy. Don't enjoy your days too much because in just a few short months your husband will be locked up, you will be raising your two girls on your own, and you will be spending your weekends driving hours each way to visit your husband in federal prison."

Last night's dinner out with Matt turned heartbreakingly emotional. We were seated at a tiny table in the basement of the Boarding House, a cozy 125-year-old watering hole and one of our favorite places to dine while on the island. We shared a decadent meal and tried to spend quality time together and reconnect. But after a drink or two, the mood turned heavy and sad. Being there seemed to represent all that was delicate and beautiful in our marriage and all that would be taken away from us within a short few months.

We began talking about the institution of marriage. I told Matt I believe marriages fall into several categories. There is the idyllic version that many girls fantasize about beginning in childhood. The sanitized Disney version where the prince rescues the princess and they live happily ever. While many long for this, I've learned that clinging to this childish fantasy more often than not ends in disillusion and divorce.

Then there are the marriages that are functional and realistic. They blend love, commitment, procreation, and partnership. Ups and downs exist, as do joy and heartbreak. There is a healthy balance between dependency and individualism. While far from perfect, this marriage is solid. The romance comes and goes, but respect for one another and for the marriage prevails over human weakness and fault. This is the kind of marriage my parents have.

Then there are the marriages that start out strong but don't function well when life's inevitable challenges arise. These stresses and strains take on a toxic, volatile quality that becomes ingrained in the fabric of the marriage. The couple's individual or joint missteps seem unforgivable. This marriage becomes combative in nature. Its original sweetness ferments over time into a hardened, withered reality. Couples in this union may or may not stay together. Some are seduced by the addictive drama of alternating love and hate, while others become utterly destroyed by it. For them, leaving the marriage seems the only path for salvation. Yet sometimes they find themselves so mired in dysfunction and codependency that they stay.

I initially believed my marriage was a genuine fairy tale. Don't we all believe or want to believe that somehow our marriage is special? That our love will conquer all? Most marriages begin with hope and open hearts, then life gets in the way.

Our marriage was complicated, like most. I started wondering if, despite the foundation of love and friendship, our marriage had become compromised beyond repair. Matt didn't see things the way I did. He saw our union as solid, adding, "What we sometimes lack in passion, we more than make up for with our unwavering commitment to one another." He said he was surprised and hurt by what he deemed as my pessimistic rant on the institution of marriage. The night ended with my alcohol-induced tears, and we didn't revisit the topic.

No one on Nantucket seems to know about Matt's indictment. This is a welcome relief. I attempt to live my days here in denial-laden bliss. While I know it isn't going to last long, for now it feels like a break. A break from the looks of pity, the phone calls, and the sometimes strained encounters with friends and neighbors. A break from the friends who are too cautious around me, reluctant to share their own problems for fear of sounding petty. Or worse, the friends who do share their current struggles only to follow up by voicing regret that they had done so. A break from the constant elephant in the room. So for now we keep our depressing story to ourselves and embrace the mirage that is our last Nantucket summer.

In mid-July, Matt and I talk about the deal he is trying to make pre-sentencing. He admits to making one bad choice. "The worst decision of my life was to go to trial instead of agreeing up front to settle with the government." He is furious his lawyer didn't make it clearer to him that by going to trial, he was essentially a dead man walking—that virtually no white-collar crime of his sort is winnable in court.

Matt's lawyer apparently lied to us when we asked her about the minimum and maximum prison time. She told us what we wanted to hear. I will never know what private conversations transpired between her and Matt, but I only can imagine she saw he was a fighter, which translated to monetary gain for her. In her defense, I don't think Matt was eager to back down from the trial because he had convinced himself of his innocence.

We are now learning that, based on a formulaic point system, Matt could be sentenced to seventeen years or more. When pressed before, Matt's lawyer said he'd likely get seven years tops. Matt and I used her inaccurate worst-case scenario of seven years to create a fantasy of a possible one- to two-year sentence. We had been hanging out in a delusional space fueled by hope, denial, and ignorance.

I am struggling to decipher what is real versus what is delusional. Matt seems to continue living in a perpetual state of denial. When something negative happens, especially by his hand, he wants to will it away. He thinks this is being positive. While positivity can be a useful quality, it becomes dysfunctional when used as an armor against truth. I desperately wish Matt would take a good, hard look at himself and admit his faults.

I want him to express his remorse. Perhaps even more than that, I want him to admit that he is flawed, that he is a mere mortal who has made terrible mistakes. I don't know how I will be able to forgive him and begin healing until he acknowledges his transgressions.

Some people have asked me why this is so important to me. Especially Matt's mom. Throughout my twenty-five years with Matt, I often have allowed my reality, my feelings, and my beliefs to be usurped by his. I often have felt oppressed by him. Not free to express opinions that differed from his and certainly not able to express dissatisfaction. Especially if my discontent was aimed toward him.

I know in my heart of hearts that Matt did not wish to cause anyone pain. But his ego got in the way of a fantastic life. He says he has no regrets about how he conducted business and how he lived his life. I feel that hubris continues to be his greatest nemesis.

Matt refuses to face his demons. His survival instinct is well honed. He will not be beaten down by what lies ahead. His "no looking back" mentality translates to "forge ahead, fight, stay strong, beat this." But sometimes one can make the same mistake over and over if they don't take an honest look in the mirror.

My emotions vacillate like this summer's fickle weather. Some days we wake to rainstorms and high winds that give way to dramatically blue skies by lunch, followed by fog in the afternoon, then back to ocean breezes and sunshine by early evening. Similarly, my heart might feel open and pure during yoga or a drive out to Bartlett's farm, then grey and cold two hours later when I am home making lunches and doing laundry, then calm and peaceful again after a swim with Ava. I try to tell myself during one of my open and light moods that I have the power to maintain this mental state. But for me, what goes up always comes down. A more practical goal for me would be to remember that when my mind becomes dark, that too shall pass. As a new day is born, the sun will rise again.

I will desperately miss our beautiful days here on Nantucket. Nothing soothes me more than the sound of the waves mixed with the smell of the sea and hints of perfume from the summer flora. I am starting to leave already as I wake each morning and peer up at the raftered ceiling then out to the sea. I count the days we have left. And I begin to mourn what will never be again. I want to absorb every last drop. As the days slip by, I try to store the memories deep within me. I want to package the quiet mornings, the calm, the good. Soon this will become one more loss.

We left Nantucket today with heavy hearts. The sky opened up as our ferry pulled away from the dock and the light drizzle turned into a torrential downpour. The chilling grey weather is sadly befitting. No one wants to leave. Eliza, who always sleeps soundly, woke up at 4 a.m. crying that she didn't want to go home. She said she doesn't like Pennsylvania. She said she wished that Nantucket could be our real home forever. As the girls threw their pennies into the Nantucket Sound with their wishes and dreams, I was crying softly as I stood behind them knowing their childhood summer home would soon be gone forever.

CHAPTER NINE

State of Our Union

Autumn 2014

Last night I had a dream that seemed to go on all night. Even after waking up to use the bathroom, the dream resumed the moment I returned to bed. Like most bad dreams, it was fear-based.

Here's the real-life context for the dream, followed by the dream itself.

The Reality: On the way to a Labor Day barbecue last night, I told Matt that as soon as he goes to prison, I am going to fire his assistant Jackie. I have pleaded with him several times over the years to let her go. I never cared for her, and I am troubled by the role she plays in his life.

For the past nine years, Jackie has helped Matt with his bookkeeping and many other logistical and personal matters. She pays bills, writes checks, and handles his schedule and travel arrangements. She is single and lives in

Center City in an apartment in the former Warwick Hotel. Matt purchased this condo as an "investment." He insisted I cosign the loan even as I protested. It was the last thing I wanted or believed we needed. Jackie lives in my apartment, and her rent covers the mortgage.

It doesn't help that she's an attractive, petite Jewish girl, who looks like me (except for the petite part). When Matt speaks to her on the phone, his voice softens and he does this little thing with his head, a tiny shaking. Then there are his eyes, which smile even when his mouth doesn't.

In the past I insecurely joked about Jackie wanting to take my place as his wife if I were to die. Matt would usually laugh it off. Sometimes he'd ask me why I was jealous of her. Once, he looked straight into my eyes and calmly said, "I wish you didn't feel that way."

Matt was never reactionary or emotional about my accusations. He also didn't fight with me on the topic, which only further supported my assumptions. Since he didn't manipulate me to believe otherwise or engage in his typical challenging or defensive manner, what did this mean? At the very least, I am certain Matt was emotionally cheating on me. I wondered if I had become complacent about their relationship because it took pressure off me to do the wifely administrative things I didn't want to do like manage our personal finances. And perhaps meet other needs as well.

The Dream: Matt and Jackie are having a full-blown affair. It has been going on for several years. I have just learned about it and am gathering clothes, food, and money so I can leave him. My girls want to know what I am doing. In the dream, the affair gets entwined with my apparent need to run from the government, taking on a Hollywood-like drama.

The news of the affair and my intended escape are leaked to the public. Suddenly I am at a party, where I continue stuffing my suitcase with clothes. I secretly take cash and credit cards from my father while trying to escape the cameras and interviewers. I find myself partly naked in a car with several of Matt's coworkers. They confirm that not only has Matt been unfaithful to me with Jackie, but that she is running the company and has become quite wealthy working with Matt.

The dream skips two years into the future, and I am still running. I am by myself. I find a photograph of Eliza and Ava. It is from one of their Bat Mitzvahs. They look so grown-up and are stunningly dressed in perfect dresses. Jackie has officially slipped into my role as their mother and is doing a better job of it than I.

I awake at 4:22 a.m. drenched in sweat. The dream is so accurately aligned with some of my core fears and insecurities that in my groggy, early morning state I cannot decipher truth from fiction. When I become more alert, I start to analyze. What I come to terms with is this: I am afraid both of losing Matt and of being dependent on Jackie to help manage our personal and family finances. I am insecure about my role as wife, and I feel bad that I am not adequately instilling more of a Jewish foundation into our daughters' lives. As a wife and as a mother, I feel like a failure.

Like all my dreams, I share this one right away with Matt. He is empathetic. Quietly he says, "Sorry, Jenn. I wish there was something I could do." As is his modus operandi when an emotionally intense subject arises, Matt assumes a preternaturally calm demeanor. Who knows what is really going on inside him? I certainly don't.

Just beneath his smooth façade, he may be feeling responsible for my fears or unhappiness, and his shame quiets him. Or, perhaps he is making a strategic decision to not feed my fire or my ire. I can't get a straight answer. His deflections (manipulations?) distract me. In the case of this dream, as in so many other instances, Matt's outwardly detached reaction leaves me questioning my own instincts.

As my forty-sixth birthday approaches, Matt and I go to the newly revitalized East Passyunk area of downtown Philadelphia for a special birthday dinner. Two Pimm's

Cups into what began as a seemingly normal evening, I throw my first verbal dagger. The combination of drinking and several hours of uninterrupted time with Matt lead me to unleash huge pockets of anger.

Ammunition is neatly lined up beneath the pores of my tanned summer skin, ready to fire when provoked. All it took to incite my rage was Matt asking my opinion about a current business deal then minutes later attempting to surreptitiously send an e-mail.

"Matt, you are guilty of the crimes you have been accused of! Admit it already! Please stop denying your role in this crooked operation!"

He looks stunned. His big blue eyes nearly fill with tears, and the expression on his face reveals a sense of betrayal. Up to this point, I have been unwaveringly supportive. I have played the role of the good wife. I have wanted to believe every word he has spoken to me. Every crafty, wordy, complicated explanation about his innocence. What he hears me say tonight at this quaint South Philly restaurant jolts him. It is clearly a turning point.

He counters. "You are not being fair or honest with yourself or with me. If you truly think I'm guilty, then you don't believe in me and can't support me. And if that's the case, you are deceiving us both by pretending otherwise at a nice French dinner celebrating your birthday."

It is the most straightforward thing he has said to me in a long time, and it leaves me breathless. Uncomfortable silence permeates the air. I feel challenged by Matt, as I often do. In blind faith, I have been supporting my husband. Now I have serious doubts about his innocence, and it breaks my heart.

While I may not know what I want from Matt or my marriage in the long-term, right now, I hunger for him to detail his transgressions. But I am not holding my breath. In the nearly twenty-five years I have known Matt, I have never heard him say, "I took an errant path" or "I was wrong." Whenever he apologizes, it is paired with defensiveness.

Matt says he does not want to look back. His only interest is in moving forward. I understand this, and I know that his attempts at self-preservation cater to his deeply rooted survival instincts. If he admits failure, he will crumble and fall. But I need and want him to take ownership of his mistakes. If he can do this, maybe I can forgive him. But he can't. I am furious he threw caution to the wind. I am concerned our lives together may be broken beyond repair.

The next day I am home alone. With last night's birthday dinner conversation lingering in my mind, I become sullen and weepy. I am scared. Suddenly, I am panicky about losing Matt. I try to convince myself that losing him to a decade or two in prison is not the same as losing him to death or divorce. He will not be gone forever. We will be able to talk to him by phone frequently. We will be able to visit him on weekends. He will still be a presence in our lives. And while he likely will be unable to attend the girls' school graduations, he should be out of prison in time to attend their weddings and the births of our grandchildren. Yet I don't find this reassuring. I just feel sick.

Life gives us what we need when we need it. As I continue to reflect on losing Matt, my cell phone rings. It is a new friend from the girls' school. She lost her husband and three small children in a devastating car accident many years ago. She was the only survivor. She went on to remarry, and she now has twin daughters in Eliza's class. Seeing her name appear on my phone puts an abrupt stop to my negative ruminations.

My loved ones are with me on this earth. My girls are my precious treasures. We are all healthy and blessed. My mind turns to my cousin Karen and her husband, Jacques, who lost their only son, Alexander, when he was a sophomore at Yale University. He was training on his road bike for a cross-country race to raise funds and awareness for Habitat for Humanity. He was hit by a truck and died instantly. Alexander was a kind, beautiful, intelligent young man. He was vibrant and loving, giving and generous. Just like that, he was taken.

Karen, Jacques, and their daughter, Katherine, personify grace, dignity, and strength in the face of tragedy. Their grieving process has been both humble and courageous. They focus their energies not on self-pity but rather on remembering their son and brother through the creation of a foundation that honors Alexander's life and provides scholarship money to a deserving Yale student with exemplary qualities. They inspire me and remind me that I am not alone on my journey. They provide me with courage and hope that I, too, can get through my pain. I aspire to mirror their strength as I travel my own road toward acceptance and peace.

Today is September 11, 2014. Thirteen years have passed since the tragedy of 9/11. Another sign. Another lesson in grace. All those families who lost their fathers, mothers, husbands, wives, sons, and daughters have somehow survived. I will not even attempt to put myself in their shoes. But I do find inspiration in their stories, their strength, their ability to forge ahead.

This morning Matt readily took the girls to school when I asked him to. Prior to today, he has never taken the children to school. Never. On the few previous occasions I asked Matt to drive the girls for me, he'd reply with a simple "no."

Matt's resistance to helping with the parenting chores was deeply rooted in resentment and power. Since I didn't contribute to or assist with the household finances and because he worked tirelessly to create a lifestyle that afforded us material luxury, he insisted I handle everything that had to do with the children. This rigid division of labor cost us all dearly. Matt lost the chance to be closer to the girls. This deprived him and them of a level of intimacy the girls deeply deserved.

I am far from blameless. I frequently enabled and reinforced this dynamic out of guilt. There were days when Matt would come home exhausted from a hard day at the office, while I had spent numerous hours and hundreds or possibly even thousands of dollars at Neiman Marcus. There were many school events I allowed him to skip so he could work or relax. I thought I was helping by "letting him off the hook," but in reality, I was depriving him and our girls of precious father-daughter bonding time.

Now that we are weeks away from Matt's incarceration, his involvement with the girls and our family life has changed dramatically. It feels warm and comforting, and the sense of togetherness is almost idyllic. It torments me that we were unable to achieve this level of parental partnership and family cohesion until we were confronted with its absence. As I watch Matt desperately try to make up for lost time, my heart bleeds for him.

During the financial crisis of 2008-2009, Matt started to slowly come back to us. It was a matter of circumstance. Because the real estate market was hit hard and deals were at a minimum, he was able to be home more often. Matt did not make much money during that period, and I know that was difficult for him. But instead of allowing financial stress dominate, we grew closer as a couple. We worked together to limit spending. For a brief period, we were a team. But once business picked up again, Matt checked back out of everyday family life. It wasn't until he was indicted that Matt began to return to us.

CHAPTER TEN

Sentencing

Autumn 2014

I don't trust that Matt is being forthcoming with me. I wish to God he didn't feel the need to hide the truth. I can only assume that his motivation comes from a place of love, but also fear. His instinct is to protect me, but he is in a constant battle, trying desperately to also protect himself. I know he dreads my disapproval and will sugarcoat reality to avoid controversy. Yet there is no cloak big or colorful enough to hide the glaring reality of what lies ahead.

Tonight when Matt came home from work and told me his sentencing has been set for October 7th, I told him I'd been praying for a late October date with the hope he might still be with us for Christmas. He said he'd been reflecting on Halloween last year, recalling that as he walked with the girls around the neighborhood he thought to himself, "If I could get just one more Halloween like this one."

That struck me as odd. Last October I was still under the impression that Matt would be able to make a deal with the government and avoid prison time. Did Matt know all along that a deal was highly unlikely? He certainly didn't present it that way to me. The combination of me not more actively seeking information about the case and Matt's desire to shelter me from pain led me to cling to false hope for far too long.

The first thought I have each morning, even before my eyes are open is, "Matt will be incarcerated very soon." I am on the verge of tears now while I listen to the girls shriek with joy as they jump on the trampoline with their father.

Matt has been deliciously involved lately. Even though it was by no means the norm before, the time and attention Matt now gives us feels natural. It's what I always dreamed of. Matt is approaching every moment as if it were a precious gift. I wish I could do the same. For me, though, every happy moment is overshadowed by impending loss.

We are a week away from sentencing. Our neighbor, Anna, is a photographer who thoughtfully offered to take family pictures of us as a gift knowing they'd be the last family photos we will be taking for years. She came over to deliver them this morning. The photographs are beautiful.

Two seconds after Anna leaves, the doorbell rings again. I'm guessing she forgot her keys but instead she tells me, "You have a news crew here."

"What? Jesus!" I reply. Dasher is barking inconsolably.

"What should I tell them?"

"Tell them I'm not here."

Anna leaves and a minute later the bell is ringing and the reporters are knocking, or rather banging, on my door. They know I am here. Poor Dasher is losing it. I text Matt and he calls me right away.

"Can you see them?" Matt asks.

"Let me peek out the window. Yeah, there are two people. Shit. They are filming now, right in the driveway."

"What kind of car do they have? Can you see the name of the network?"

"I don't want to look out again. I don't want them to see me."

"Just peek out one more time."

"No!" I run around and shut the shades. "You need to pick up the kids from school today. I am not leaving the house with them out there."

"Okay. I will. Maybe I need to hire a security guard, our road is private … assholes."

"I'm closing the front curtains."

"No, don't. You don't want them to think that you are hiding."

"I am hiding."

After about ten minutes of filming and attracting the attention of curious neighbors who were drawn to linger nearby, the news team left. I later heard from friends that on the 10 p.m. news that night, a short report on Matt's impending sentencing and incarceration aired.

I am exhausted by the intense mood swings I've been experiencing lately. It feels like I am wearing a heavy coat I can't shed. Sometimes the coat is well suited for the chilly weather, and I briefly settle into a state of almost coziness. But soon thereafter, the temperature rapidly rises. The coat is heavy and oppressive, but I can't take it off.

Today's heartache comes in the form of a thick manila envelope from the probation officer. It includes a lengthy summation of the indictment, trial, family history, work history, and Matt's basic life story. While there are no major surprises, reading it makes me nauseous. When I call Matt to share what I have read, my disdain cannot be masked.

"Is there anything in there you like?" he asks. Sadly I know he means it. His ego continues to hold him at arm's length from the truth.

"Not a thing."

Matt, ever hopeful, is trying to cling to any glimmer of positivity. I simultaneously am furious with and feel sorry for him. At this point, I don't know if it matters what the truth is or what is in the report.

Four days before Matt's sentencing is Yom Kippur. The holiest and most revered of all the Jewish holidays, the Day of Atonement. I will fast for twenty-four hours. I will pray and repent for all my sins from the past year. I want to ask for forgiveness for Matt's sins as well. But how can I ask others to forgive him when I can't? I am told that his transgressions are not my cross to bear, but if he is not taking responsibility, does the burden not trickle down to me? His wife for better or for worse.

I am scared to face parenting alone. I am distraught knowing the girls will grow up without a father. I do not feel strong enough to pull this off. In a recent moment of desperation, I entertained a plan for our entire family to flee the country. A friend whose husband is in jail for one year gave me this idea. I seriously consider it. She tells me that Israel would take us, and that maybe she could even help arrange a private plane to get us there.

She stares at me with huge serious and loving eyes and urges, "This is your family, Jennifer." I talk to Matt's mother about the idea. She thinks it is a good one. We're both coming more from a place of fear than reason. I discuss the possibility with Matt. He talks me out of it. The risk is too great he tells me. I'd be a criminal too, he says, and the girls could end up losing both parents. Of course he's right. But I worry that later I will regret this choice.

October 7th. The long anticipated day of sentencing has arrived. Walking into the courtroom with Matt and his parents is like re-entering a bad dream. I am surprised to see the benches are already filled with so many of our friends and family. It is only 9:30 a.m., and the court session won't begin until 10 a.m. I am overwhelmed with emotion and gratitude. I hug everyone briefly and do my best to keep from losing it. I can't utter a word. I take my place on the front bench next to my sister Kim.

The judge walks in looking tired and slightly disoriented. Everyone stands. He tells us to be seated. He puts his glasses on and looks down at his notes briefly, then starts to address the court. I remember very little of what he says. I do remember praying hard. Like a little girl who wants to be picked for a team, saying over and over in my head, "Please, please, please, please, please go easy on him."

He invites Matt to address the court. Matt is shaking as he walks up to the front of the room and takes the stand. He pulls out his prepared notes from his pocket. He tells the court that he is sorry. He asks the judge to consider his family. Me and the girls. That is all.

Next I remember the judge announcing that Matt would be sentenced to 5,840 days in prison and to report on Jan 7, 2015. Blood rushes loudly in my ears as I hear someone say, "Sixteen years."

Matt starts to cry. He walks over to us and tells his mother he is sorry. Everyone is crying. My friend Janine reassures me she will continue to be there for me. I can't look at my family. Jackie is sitting next to me. She turns to face me and says, "I am so sorry."

I go into the bathroom and am crying hysterically. My mom and sister Courtenay hug me as they cry. When we emerge, Matt's brother Kieran gives me a long hug, saying I am his sister and he will be there for me. Matt's brother Ryan hugs me and says, "We're gonna get through this." Matt's uncle Tim tells me he loves me.

I honestly don't remember where Matt was in those moments. The next thing I recall we are all standing in the lobby, with everyone in a state of disbelief. Matt's three best friends, Guntie, Henrick, and Mark, are standing together surrounding Matt, all with red eyes. No one knows what to say. No one wants to leave. For some, it is the last time they will see Matt.

Sentenced to sixteen years in prison. Accounting for good behavior, the earliest Matt likely can be released is thirteen years. By then, Eliza will be twenty-five, Ava will be twenty-three, and Matt and I will both be fifty-nine. It's incomprehensible.

YOU HAVE TWELVE NEW VOICE MESSAGES:

"Hi … uh … It's your neighbor, Irma. I was just walking the dog, I'm in your cul-de-sac … I walk him at night. I just wanted to say that I'm here for you if you need anything. Well okay, call me."

"Hi Jenn, it's me, Kristin. I wanted to see if you wanted to talk. You probably don't yet. Let me know what I can do, anything. A meal, if you need help with the girls. I'll do anything. Oh Jenn, I'm sorry, so sorry." Her voice cracked. She was clearly crying.

"Hey Jenn, it's Melissa. I just read your e-mail. This is totally unfair. Let me know what I can do. When does he go? Please give Matt a big hug for me and call me when you feel like talking. Love you girl. Stay strong."

"Hi, it's Suz calling again. I just want you to know that you will always have a friend in me. I am here for you whenever you are ready."

"Jenn? It's Maureen. I don't know what to say. Call me if you want to take a walk or when you feel like talking. Can I do anything?"

"Hey babe, it's Iris. Your phone is off. Call me and let me know if there is anything I can do. Or don't call me, I love you."

"Hey Jenn, it's Kim. I didn't expect you to pick up. I just want to let you know that I'm here for you and that I'm sorry about the sentencing. I'm here for you in any way you need me. Love you."

"It's Care, I am here for you. Please let me know what I can do. I am only two hours away. I love you both so much, and we are all thinking of you every second down here. I don't want to pester you, but please know that I'll do anything, ANYTHING!"

"Hey Jenn, it's Kieran. It is very early on the West Coast, and I was thinking of you. I just wanted to hear your voice. I love you. Give a call."

I also receive a barrage of e-mails, which tended to be lengthier and more intimate. The texts are candid and straightforward.

I do not pick up the phone. It is so hard to talk. I am actually scared to answer the phone. Afraid I will have to say something. Afraid of the awkwardness. Afraid of the pain and love in the voice at the other end. Afraid of my silence and tears.

Yet I want the calls, texts, and e-mails to keep coming in. What if everyone starts to leave me alone and I am left with my isolation? My thoughts are thick and cloudy. I tell myself over and over, "You will be a single parent." Yet when I try to feel what that might be like, I can't feel much.

I begin to pretend that Matt is already gone. I start to distance myself. I weep silently, alone in bed, when everyone is at school and work. It is the only place where I find comfort. When I imagine the girls growing up without their dad, my heart crumbles. I feel physically sick and depressed and near panic when I think about a future that does not include Matt.

CHAPTER ELEVEN

Elusive Grace

Winter 2008 to Present

Yoga has changed my life. As my fortieth birthday approached in 2008, I was out of shape, weak, and low in energy. I had never been a gym person nor was I generally drawn to exercise aside from the occasional ski trip, hike, or bike ride. My girls were six and four and both in school full-time, and I was greatly in need of a physical outlet. I had tried the Cricket Club tennis team for a year, but after throwing out my back and realizing my competitive side turned me into a monster, I quit.

My first months of yoga were challenging, rewarding, frustrating, and humbling in equal measure. I could barely maintain the downward dog position, which is supposed to be a resting pose. I had three steadfast and encouraging teachers who taught me about grace, balance, patience, and perseverance. It was the first time in a very long while that I felt satisfied and encouraged by a physical activity.

I was in awe of the limber seventy-year-old woman who frequently practiced near me. I was smitten with my talented teacher Robin. Although she pushed me in ways that led me to occasionally send visual daggers in her direction, I continued attending her class. Eventually I started to experiment with a large selection of practice styles, including Bikram, hot yoga, Kirtan, call and response yoga, Vinyasa, Restorative, Yin, Kundalini, and Acro.

What began as a love-hate relationship blossomed into a full-blown love affair. For the past nine years, I have consistently practiced yoga and can't imagine my life without it. Yoga has become my go-to therapy. The sense of calm and peace I feel when I am on my mat comforts and energizes me like nothing else. The music, movement, and never-ending effort to master the poses foster an internal stillness that I otherwise find difficult to access. I am grateful to my kula (community of fellow practitioners) and my gifted teachers.

I am learning that no matter how much I practice the asanas (physical poses), all that truly matters is practicing kindness. I have a really hard time with this. I try every day. And every day I have a setback. I am tired all the time and angry inside. My anger at my husband manifests itself as impatience with my children.

As I lie in bed with the doors open, the summer breeze helps soothe me as I write. It is morning, and I love the quiet solitude and peace that writing provides. Sleepy, sweet Ava comes into my room and climbs into bed with me. She is very curious about this book I'm writing. She wants to be in it and asks me to read her a part where she is the focus. I had a choice to make when she walked into my room. I was knee-deep in my creative process when she jumped onto my bed and wanted to talk and see what I was doing. My protective, guarded, selfish side wanted to shut my laptop and tell her that Mommy was working now. Instead, I am thankful my loving, open, kind side took over. I let her snuggle in next to me and ask me questions about my book. My yoga teachers guide me, but it's my children who lead me to joy and love every day. Just one tiny drop of kindness has a huge impact on Ava. She is easily satisfied. She is a gift to me in this moment and always.

Every book I read on spirituality, yoga, and Eastern philosophy teaches about the grace of acceptance. I have no idea how to get to that place of freedom. I am instructed to be present, let go, and act with kindness to oneself, the earth, and all living creatures. I struggle with this practice as I try to forgive myself and others.

I am told to be patient and grounded. Yet I am also guided to *feel* my broken heart and be at peace with the pain and the circumstances. I am taught to give to and connect with others and to avoid addictive behaviors as a strategy for coping with stress. Not to hide behind and cover up what feels unbearable. Not to numb. I am guilty of turning to food and shopping. Both acts of indulgence give me comfort. I am learning that addictions come in many forms.

All of these teachings resonate with me. While I am learning and practicing yoga, I feel empowered and at peace. But I struggle when I try to apply these fundamentals to my daily life. So many times I walk out of yoga class with a smile on my face, my body relaxed, my mind at peace.

I remind myself, "This is you, Jennifer. This is pure. This is your best self. Be kind and patient when you walk into your beautiful home, and let the day unfold in peace." Sometimes I don't even make it upstairs before I feel my temperature starting to rise. Annoyed at what? The house not being clean? The family enjoying a lazy Sunday? Why should these things make me crazy? Make me start yelling? In yoga I feel strong and in control of my body and mind. In life I feel the opposite.

The path to wise action can be very long. I would like to believe I am a better person now than I was twenty years ago. But plenty of old, comfortable yet unproductive habits remain. I am teaching myself how to make malas.

They are beautiful Tibetan prayer beads, not too dissimilar from the rosary. Typically worn around the neck, malas consist of 108 semiprecious stones. Each stone carries with it unique healing or spiritual intentions. Meant to assist in meditation, mala beads have been appearing well beyond the yoga studio.

I have admired these beautiful necklaces for the past several years. One of my beloved yoga teachers on Nantucket started making mala jewelry a few winters ago when his partner committed suicide. I am inspired by this gifted yoga teacher who has become a talented jeweler. He said the practice of the simple and repetitive beadwork settled him and helped heal his heart. I am hoping for the same outcome.

I watch several YouTube videos to learn the seemingly simple beading technique. I give up after an hour. I do not have all the materials. For a few minutes, I beat myself up. I know I will come back to this project. Perhaps the grace in my "mala moment" is that I am beginning to better understand my limits. I need to take breaks often. Shift gears. Then return. I know I am easily overwhelmed and discouraged. I am learning to not criticize myself as much. Sometimes it is nearly impossible, as my inner voice usually says, "What's wrong with you?" I even hear myself say out loud, "I hate myself." I am trying to change this. To not self-deprecate. To not give up or give in to the feeling of helplessness. To circle back to my goals.

I want to change my internal wiring. Sometimes I think it is impossible. My muscle memory is so ingrained, so habitual. My hope is to persevere in the middle of a challenge and not need as many time-outs. I am as aware of my negative behavior patterns as I am of my growing healthy tendencies. And I know that every minute of life is a new opportunity for goodness. Every day, probably twenty times or more, I promise myself that I will use my time wisely. That I will recognize the gifts of the day. My intentions are always good. But inevitably real life intervenes and it seems like my efforts are wasted.

"You make it miserable for everyone when you are in a bad mood! Just stop, Mommy," Eliza pleads. These are almost the identical words I spoke to her earlier in the day when we were at a pumpkin patch, and she refused to get out of the car to join us to pick pumpkins and take photos. Like all children, Eliza learns from her parents. It is frightening to see how she imitates my negative behaviors. I am humbled that my morning's pledge of kindness has been so quickly put to the test. I witness myself handling it poorly as I yell at her to get out of the car and join us.

Later that same day, I am awoken from a nap when Eliza walks into my bedroom. Before I am out of bed, I hear myself instinctually barking out orders.

"Eliza, do your homework!"

"Not now." She had repeated this about four times since 11 a.m. I was going to put a stop to that right now.

"Eliza, do your goddamned homework now! I am so disappointed in you. You save everything for the last minute. I am not going to help you study at 9 p.m. … Never mind. Do whatever you want. Do you want to get put on academic suspension? Do you want to get kicked out of school? I am going to yoga now."

Before I leave, I manage to yell to Ava, "Get off the sofa. Clean up your crumbs and food wrappers and take poor Dasher out for a walk. He has been neglected all day!"

This is a common end-of-the-weekend pattern. We tend to be lazy on Sundays, and by the afternoon our house is a wreck. Dasher inevitably has peed on the tile floor of the girls' bathroom because he wasn't taken out enough. Ava watches too much TV while eating snacks, which makes a mess on the sofa. Eliza has not touched her weekend homework.

After I yell, I leave for yoga. By the time I come home, Eliza has done most of her homework, and Ava took Dasher out for five minutes. It's not much, but it's better than nothing. For the moment, I am calm.

Yesterday I had the good fortune of meeting with a woman whose husband currently is serving an eight-month sentence at Fort Dix Prison in New Jersey. My friend Iris had given me her number several times, and because I finally felt the need to "check that box," I e-mailed her. We set up a time to meet at her home. We ended up talking for three hours.

It was the first time since Matt's indictment that I have felt completely understood. While her situation varies from mine in several ways, those differences proved to be inconsequential. I immediately felt like I was talking with a best friend. I let her soothe me with comforting words and miso soup. She described in detail what the visits were like. She shared her pain about feeling misunderstood by her friends and family. At one point her sixteen-year-old daughter came into the kitchen. When she told her daughter that my husband was going to prison and that I had two daughters, her daughter started to cry.

What meant the most was how genuine this woman was with me. She was gentle and caring and understanding. She listened, she cried, she advised, she shared, and she gave me a glimmer of hope that I, too, could survive my husband's incarceration.

CHAPTER TWELVE

Assigned to Allenwood

Autumn 2014

While Eliza and I are out doing errands, I receive a text from Matt stating simply, "I am being sent to Allenwood." My initial reaction is to blurt out, "Oh my God!" and tell Eliza I need to call Daddy. She asks, "Is Ava okay? Did she break her leg at Sky Zone?"

I quickly Google "Allenwood" and learn that the Allenwood Federal Correctional Complex is comprised of low, medium, and high security prisons, which cumulatively house approximately 2,900 inmates. Matt is being sent to Allenwood's low security prison. The Complex is a three-hour drive from here, and visiting hours are only on Fridays, Saturdays, and Sundays.

A few days later, I receive a text from Matt that reads, "Rough day. Coming home now." My heart sinks. I never used to receive texts like this from him. Not because he didn't have plenty of rough days; he did. It's just that we didn't text each other to check in. I'd typically detect a stressful day either by his mood or a volatile phone conversation he'd be having with a client as he walked in the door. I also have never known stress or illness to cause Matt to come home early from work.

Now we act like grown-ups. Like partners. When I receive this text, I am terrified. I'm thinking, "How can this get worse?" Yet I know it can. We are completely powerless over our lives. Our government has spoken, the jury has spoken, and anything can be taken from us. I wonder if Matt's hard day has something to do with our Nantucket house, which we "gave up" in exchange for a lesser prison sentence. Perhaps his rough day has to do with another blow regarding our finances.

We no longer have money. Our joint account is in the negative. My individual savings account of $13,000 will be rapidly gobbled up by our monthly living expenses. I am making spending money by selling our things to strangers through eBay and to friends and neighbors through Facebook. I am purging my jewelry, furniture, our piano, the ping-pong table. Also, Christmas is coming. While I don't mind getting rid of most of these things, what stings is the reason I am in this position. I am angry we didn't plan better and that every last penny of our savings went to lawyers, and it didn't help us.

It is so hard not to look back and think of all the things that could have been done differently. It is hard not to place blame. We have so little time left together as a family before Matt reports for prison. Although I try to normalize our days, each moment feels burdened by significance. I feel guilty when I do not make every second count. I think about what one of my yoga teachers says right before Shavasana at the end of each class. She tells us to take a moment for ourselves and use it wisely because once it is gone, we can't get it back. The clock is ticking. If I squander even one minute with Matt or spend it feeling angry with him, or waste time by not doing lovely family things, I end up mired in regret.

There is a fine line between compassion and pity. I do not want anyone feeling sorry for me, ever. I don't think people mean to do it, but nonetheless the sound in their voices and the look in their eyes reveal the truth.

I saw two dear, longtime friends last week. Each was amazingly sensitive and helpful. One cried and told me she is worried. This made me feel loved and held in ways I can't explain. The other friend asked a handful of practical questions, which helped me verbalize difficult thoughts and feelings about what was happening. I did not feel the need to protect myself. Being with each of them was a salve.

With Christmas, Hanukah, and Ava's birthday on the horizon, the girls are getting excited. We are happily distracted with baking and readying the house for the holidays. I think, "How strange. To be happy and content despite knowing what lies ahead." I don't think it is denial. I really don't know what it is. Is it acceptance? Or perhaps conditional acceptance? In this moment at least, I seem to be able to enjoy feeling good while also being aware that feeling awful awaits me.

We may be functioning better as a family than we ever have before. The irony is thick and somewhat sickening. Tonight Ava asked me if we'd be able to return to our Nantucket home. I told her I thought there was a chance. Matt is working hard to make a deal with the government for the rights to be able to sell it on our own. Our hope is that we could sell it to someone we know personally, and in exchange for giving the buyer a good deal, the girls and I could rent it back on a yearly basis for three weeks in July and for the week of Christmas.

Once the girls were in bed, Matt had a more pointed question.

"Are you considering divorcing me?"

This takes me surprise. I cautiously reply, "Why would I do that?"

"So that you could remarry and not have to be alone."

"I wouldn't do that to the kids or to you."

"Consider yourself, Jenny."

"I will never remarry, even if you were to die. I no longer believe that marriage suits me."

At this stage in my life, the institution of marriage is useless to me. It has served its purpose. I was conditioned to be coupled, and I craved that union. I wanted to marry Matt and create our family. Now I have a husband, a marriage, and our girls, yet my husband is being taken from me. I have neither the need nor desire to do it all over again.

While Matt's question may have caught me off guard, I have been incessantly contemplating life without him. I will sorely miss Matt, perhaps unbearably so at times. His question was valid, and I have no clue how I will fill the void of his absence.

I recently asked my friend Maureen who is a divorced mother of two children if she wants to marry again. She tells me that she is happy, actually thrilled, by her solo lifestyle. She loves that her free time is hers alone. She prefers it that way. Although our circumstances are quite different, I can't help but wonder if I will feel the same way.

With good behavior and a year in a halfway house, Matt's sixteen-year sentence could be reduced to thirteen. Yet thirteen years is still a very long time. I can't imagine spending the next thirteen years driving three hours each way every other weekend to spend a couple of hours with

Matt. Is this how it will be for us until Eliza is twenty-five and Ava is twenty-three, or until each one goes to college? What are we all going to be like on the other end of this? Bitter? Hardened? Strong? Ah yes, well at least we will be strong—at least 4,745 days stronger.

Eliza was punished tonight. We took her phone away, and Matt put her to bed early. I haven't seen him this angry with her in a long time. The triggering incident happened when I picked her up from a new friend's house.

Her friend's family had guests over with whom they were about to sit down for dinner. Before Eliza and I headed out, I mentioned to her friend's mother that I'd like to have their daughter over for a sleepover at our house. Since Hebrew school is on Sunday mornings, we agreed that most Saturday nights were less than optimal. We then talked about some mutual friends' Bat Mitzvah dates, and I said that Eliza wouldn't be having a Bat Mitzvah. Eliza chimed in, "Of course I won't be having one because I am not frickin' Jewish!"

I was mortified. The other couple and the girl's father looked over, and I thought I might die right there. On the way home, I tried to explain how wrong and hurtful her comment was. I told her that most Jews, including myself, take pride in their religion, and to comment negatively about anyone's religion is inappropriate and intolerant.

I think she was starting to get it, but when we got home and I told Matt, she heard it again from him.

Eliza has been on an "I'm not Jewish" tirade for about a year now. She is using the mixed marriage card as a cop-out, saying that any religion that celebrates Christmas is the way to go. Although we are raising the girls in the Jewish faith, we continue to celebrate and honor the McManus family's tradition of Christmas. To try to offset the inevitable confusion of an interfaith family, we tell our girls we are raising them Jewish and we are a Jewish family. We've explained that Matt was raised Catholic, but that we made the decision together to be "religiously" a Jewish family.

Nonetheless, Eliza claims that she flat out does not want to be Jewish or have anything to do with Judaism. She has gone as far as to reject any Chanukah gifts that come her way. If I look at her reasoning in simplistic, black-and-white terms, she is choosing to align with Christianity because Christmas is fun. But nothing Eliza thinks or does is black-and-white. She has been a complex girl from the day she was born. She is an old soul, with more going on inside than meets the eye.

Perhaps she just doesn't "feel" Jewish. With her blond hair, blue eyes, and fair skin, she looks much more like her Irish relatives than her Jewish ones. Maybe she is embarrassed by her Judaism, as there are very few Jews at

Germantown Academy and in our neighborhood. Maybe the denouncement of her religion is an expression of her naturally contrarian nature. Or maybe she is rebelling against me. We always have had a complicated relationship, and we are opposites in many ways. Whatever the reason, I have learned to accept her wishes. At first I tried to resist. Tried to force it, tried to reason with her, tried to make Hanukah as fun as Christmas.

Matt and I have challenged the seeming superficiality of her espoused perspective to no avail. But to humiliate me and talk the way she did at her friend's house is unacceptable. Far more than preteen sassiness, Eliza's words struck at a deep personal and intergenerational wound. I felt like she was contributing to the centuries of anti-Semitism that have plagued the Jews. This is not the first time that she has said something derogatory about being Jewish, just never before in public.

Eliza's stubbornness, tenacity, and defiance concern me. Just yesterday Matt and I were commenting on how mature she is becoming. Tonight Matt asked me where her vitriol comes from. He must be joking. Her strong personality runs fiercely down both parental bloodlines. Eliza is clearly acting out, and I am afraid of how Matt's incarceration will affect her already challenging persona.

I am not ready for Matt to leave. I don't feel capable surviving this loss. When I would picture Matt dying an early death from lung cancer, for example, I would imagine myself in bed for weeks, maybe months. Not being able to face my life without him. How will his departure to prison manifest itself for me? How depressed will I become and for how long?

I continue to worry we are not optimally using the time we have left together. Tonight I feel guilty that I didn't go with Matt to the girls' gymnastics practice. We could have had that time together in the car, or maybe gone out for a drink, or just sat on the bench together and watched our talented daughters and kvelled. Instead I stay home to isolate. Alone with my pain, I anxiously clean the kitchen, do laundry, and begin organizing for Ava's tenth birthday party.

This weekend fourteen girls will add joy and distraction to our home while we celebrate Ava's double digits and decorate gingerbread houses. It will be loud and crazy fun, and they will all sleep over. Matt of course will be a hit, with his wildness, piggyback rides, and his famous scary stories before bed.

As Matt's incarceration date rapidly approaches, I initiate many conversations with the girls about him leaving. We briefly discuss details such as how often we will visit him and what we will do next year over the holidays when he is not with us. Our conversations tend to be short and practical. While I continue to raise the topic, I can't force the girls to talk. I wonder what is going on in the hearts and minds of my precious preteens whose Daddy is going to prison next month.

The girls have had a lot of time to process the fact that he is going away. Yet like most children (and for that matter, many adults), they don't seem to want to focus on uncomfortable future events. They are in the here and now. I imagine that after we visit him for the first time and when it sinks in that he will not be a part of our daily lives, they will process this at a whole other level.

My pain is not well hidden. My face bears the lines and expression of deep anguish. I find some relief in my yoga practice, but my wise teacher sees beneath the surface. She asks me if I'm okay. I tell her I am, but I say it in such a way that she knowingly responds with compassion and understanding. It is what I need, and I leave class with a heavy heart.

I find strength in Oriah Mountain Dreamer's poem, *The Invitation.* I find myself returning to these passages, "I want to know if you have touched the center of your own sorrow, if you have been opened by life's betrayals, or have become shriveled and closed from fear of further pain. … I want to know if you can get up after the night of grief and despair, weary and bruised to the bone, and do what needs to be done to feed the children. I will not shrink and fade and let my sorrow get the better of what little life I have left ... I am bruised to the bone, but every day I will do what is required. What is important to make this life and the lives of my children and husband meaningful. I can sit with my pain, and not hide from it. To be alone with oneself, in those empty moments, and to like your own company."

While my inner world is raw and open, my external world is filled with the practicalities of our precarious financial situation. I field phone calls from debt collectors and try to borrow money from friends to catch up on overdue mortgage payments. We haven't paid our credit card bills in months.

Matt borrowed money from his best friend to pay some of his legal fees. We have reviewed our projected monthly expenses with a microscope. We have applied for financial aid at the girls' school. Matt has some pending business deals that hopefully will close in the next few months and generate income. But it won't be nearly enough to cover what we owe. For the first time in my life, money anxiety has replaced financial ignorance and lavishness. I do not have a plan. I feel unequipped to financially support myself and the girls.

Once Matt is gone, I will continue the effort to pay off our debts. I will sell every last piece of furniture and every item in my closet if I have to. He thinks I am being idealistically arrogant when I tell him I will make these payments when he is gone whether he sanctions them or not. He thinks it's okay to not pay certain people. He seems to have a business model in his head that is based on a hierarchy of needs. We owe money to the banks for our houses, to the credit card companies, to the car dealerships, to the school, to the landscaper, the pool guy, the caretaker in Nantucket. Not to mention Matt's best friend and both sets of our parents.

He claims that people don't always pay him as promised (common in the real estate deal-making world, according to him), so if he can't pay other people then well somehow "that's business." And if the "other people" he can't pay include the bank for our mortgage, then so be it. That is crazy! I am furious with him for letting our finances get this out of control, and angry with myself for not paying closer attention.

In addition to the legal and practical problems inherent in Matt's proposed approach to bill paying or rather avoidance of bill paying, I object on basic ethical grounds. It's simply wrong, and it is not the message I want to send to our daughters. Soon they will be old enough to understand this whole mess. I intend to do my best to dig our family out of the financial hole Matt has left us in. I don't yet know how or when I'll be able to do it, but I am determined to find a way.

Repaying the victims of New Realty Capital's dealings is another matter. My understanding is that the victims are collectively owed more than $26 million. Only a small percentage of the victims requested reimbursement. I'm not sure how the government is handling this, but I'm guessing those victims will be paid first. I don't know where this money will come from aside from the roughly $10 per month that Matt and his other partners expect to make "working" in prison.

As Matt's incarceration date nears, we are miraculously holding it together. There are moments of sadness and crying. The kids are fully engaged in their last weekend of winter break, distracted by a gymnastics competition on Sunday. They seem oblivious as to how their lives are about to change.

I wonder if we should stay in bed all day, savoring every last moment together as a family. But habit and routine take over. Everyday tasks are occasionally interrupted by moments of heartbreak, depression, disbelief, and worry. I also seem to find time for regret, self-pity, self-loathing, and panic.

I continually try to ground myself and consider what Matt is going through. Last night after the girls went to bed, Matt and I just sobbed and hugged and talked. We tried to comfort one another, be strong, and find meaning in this madness.

Everything I do is smothered with significance, especially the mundane. As I fold Matt's clothes, for example, I can't help thinking, "This is the last time I will launder that shirt." Then I wonder, "What should he wear when he reports to prison?" knowing of course he will be "donating" the clothes off his back as soon as he arrives.

I try to stop thinking about how this will be the last time Matt does this or that particular thing, especially when it pertains to the girls. It's simply too painful. I also try not to think too hard about what I should or should not be doing or feeling. I am in a perpetual state of unease. I feel so sensitive, so exposed, as if one misinterpreted word or one small touch will burn my skin.

In less than twenty-four hours, Matt and I will drive into the Pocono Mountains and down across Route 80 to the small town of White Deer, Pennsylvania, home of the Allenwood Federal Prison Complex. This morning I read about a woman who is turning 101 years old. Seventy years ago, she was a prisoner at the Auschwitz concentration camp in Nazi Germany. After being there for many months, she was ordered to take off her clothes and was marched into a gas chamber. She knew she was about to be incinerated. Yet when she arrived, she was told they had just run out of gas. Her life was spared. Reading about the atrocities she endured, and that she continued to create a meaningful life for seventy more years, gave me a boost of courage and hope. Maybe it will be enough to get through the next few hours or days with grace.

Tonight is our last evening as a family. Ava asks me if I think I might cry all day tomorrow. For the first time in weeks, she asks me question after question about the facility, "Is it co-ed? Will Daddy have fun there? Can we bring Dasher to visit?" She also asks me who I think will be the saddest tomorrow and declares that she's going to be the saddest for Daddy. Her compassion at such a young age is otherworldly. When I tell Eliza I am going to miss Daddy, she tells me to "suck it up." I laugh. That's one way of dealing with the pain, and sometimes it's damn efficient.

The girls stay close to us until their bedtime. As Matt puts them to bed, he spends a long time with each, rubbing their backs and cuddling for the last time. My heart breaks.

On the eve of my husband's incarceration, I find comfort in my parents' incredible generosity and compassion. (Perhaps Ava's kindness doesn't derive from another world after all.) My parents have arranged for their accountant to deposit enough money each month into my bank account to cover our mortgage and bills while I get back on my feet. My parents are doing everything possible to soften the blow and make life as smooth as possible for me and the girls. Anyone who knows them well understands that they wouldn't have it any other way. They are the most giving and supportive parents, and I am beyond grateful. They give from the bottom of their hearts. This is who they are. They are givers and helpers and the most generous people I know.

CHAPTER THIRTEEN

Freedom Lost

January 2015

The day I take my husband to prison begins the strangest, longest week of my life. At 7:45 a.m. on Tuesday, January 6th, my parents ring our doorbell. They have come from Maryland to be with the girls, who were promised a day off from school to mourn the loss of their Daddy. Matt wakes Ava and Eliza and cuddles with them in their beds for the last time ever. When Matt becomes a free man again, the girls will be in their twenties.

Ava is wailing in anguish. Eliza is hovering close to her. Matt is losing it. He is standing in the middle of the hall, crying and looking lost and childlike as I usher him out the door and into the car. I run back upstairs to reassure the girls we will all be okay, and I leave them crying together in Ava's bed, hugging Dasher and each other for comfort. My parents are softly crying in the family room, giving us our space. They hug Matt, then he and I walk out the door.

The ride to Allenwood seems like a bad dream. Matt drives. Little is said. My heart is in a painful knot, and I can't breathe properly. It is sleeting and windy. We stop for gas thirty minutes outside of White Deer. As we get off the highway and approach the tiny town where Allenwood is located, Matt's anxiety is palpable. I look at him and tell him he will be okay. "I don't want to go Jenny," is all he is able to say.

We drive up the long road that leads to the prison "campus." At first it is hardly recognizable as a prison, but soon the shining tangle of barbed wire presents itself. I feel sick. We park and walk into the lobby. At a desk sits a man who asks us how he can help. Matt tells him who he is, and the guard gets on the phone and makes a call. A minute later another guard shows up and has Matt empty his pockets. Matt hands me the car keys, his wallet, and his glasses.

Matt tells me he feels detached, like he's in a dream. I am helpless. His vulnerability is excruciating to witness. His fragility makes me love him more as I hug and reassure him.

I am under the impression that I will go with Matt to the "next step" to be further checked in. Instead the guard looks at me as if he's annoyed and I should know better.

"You won't be going anywhere." He tells us to step aside and to take a minute to say our goodbyes.

It is tearful and quick. Matt tells me he loves me, and I tell him to stay strong. Then I leave. I cry the entire snowy, sleety car ride home. I pull up to the house as the sun is beginning to set. My parents are on the sofa. There is a fire crackling in the fireplace. I hurry upstairs to hug the girls. My parents then fill me in on the day, which sounds like an average but quietly somber day. The girls stopped crying right after Matt and I left.

The next day I wake up crying and basically don't stop all day. I cry while driving the kids to school, getting new tires on my truck, going to yoga, and walking the dog. My heart is broken, my soul is screaming. It hurts physically. Somehow I do what needs to be done.

Matt calls us at 5 p.m. that evening. The three of us and Dasher huddle around the phone. It feels like we are being reunited with Matt after being apart for months, not twenty-four hours. It is a tremendous relief to hear his voice.

I can't ask him anything too difficult because the girls won't let me take him off speakerphone. They are the ones asking question after question. What are his roommates like, what kind of bed does he have, and what treats did he buy at the commissary? He sounds good. He sounds calm, relieved to have made it through the anxiety of the initial unknown.

Matt describes the atmosphere as "mellow and college-like." I am surprised by his choice of words. He explains that the institution is run with military precision in terms of cleanliness, mealtimes, and daily routine. Matt has more freedom than he anticipated with respect to making phone calls and using the computer. He is allowed to communicate by e-mail with a preapproved list of thirty family members and friends, and he describes that privilege as his lifeline. He already refers to some other inmates as friends. After we hang up, the girls skip around the kitchen, and I am all but bouncing off the walls. I am so relieved he is okay. We discuss the conversation in great detail over dinner.

Some of the girls' questions are rather sophisticated, and I am impressed by how deeply they have been thinking about everything. Ava asks if it costs money to keep Daddy in prison. She has more questions about the length of his sentence. It may have been a mistake to let the girls know we have hired a new lawyer to attempt a sentence reduction. Ava wants to know percentages and facts, and I provide her with a hypothetical range.

I spend day three at the bank, with the notary, and at Fed Ex, completing the paperwork to sell our Nantucket home. I am anxious for the sale to close smoothly, and I pray that the buyer is a man of his word and will allow us to rent the house for three weeks next summer.

On Matt's fifth day in prison, he calls and says he has bad news. In the second it takes me to go into my office and shut the door, I come up with just one scenario. Is he being relocated? My heart sinks when he tells me his e-mail privilege has been revoked. He cries as he explains that his assigned counselor told him a clerical error had been made, and because he had been charged with wire fraud with the use of a computer, the e-mail privilege should never have been granted in the first place.

This is the first time my husband sounds like what I imagine someone who is incarcerated might sound like—defeated and hopeless. Until now, he had been adjusting really well. He seemed to be accepting his fate. He was following all the rules, making friends, doing what was needed to be an ideal prisoner. He quickly established a routine that was working for him. Between meals and his job cleaning the gym facility, he'd participate in whatever group activity was presented to him. When he had unstructured time, he'd write long, thoughtful e-mails to me and the girls, and to his and my parents. Then he'd read. The highlight of his day was receiving e-mails from his friends and family.

I inform Matt's list of thirty that he can no longer be in touch by e-mail. My father, who has been beyond amazing throughout this process, immediately calls both lawyers. They say they are "working on it." Maybe it can be reversed, but that may take a year or years.

Meanwhile, more unanticipated bad news arrives that week. I am bombarded with unexpected bills and calls from debt collectors. My father is as surprised and angry as I. Matt was not up front with either of us. I think my husband might be a pathological liar.

There is no way Matt could have believed he had all his ducks in a row. Did he assume my father would pick up the pieces? I was also getting mail and calls from lawyers for lawsuits I knew nothing about. And from reporters from a television show called *American Greed.* I even had a surprise visit from a police officer who served me papers relating to the foreclosure of our apartment in Philadelphia. When I told Matt, his response was, "You didn't accept the papers, did you? You didn't sign?" Even from prison, Matt was trying to beat the system.

CHAPTER FOURTEEN

First Prison Visit

January 2015

Arriving at Allenwood with Eliza and Ava on a freezing cold but sunny January morning, my heart is pumping hard and my adrenaline is flowing. I am anxious about seeing Matt. I don't know what to expect other than what I have read from the handbook. And I am putting on a game face for the girls.

I have been hyper nervous the entire morning, throwing things into bags and getting dressed in the most appropriately casual yet conservative outfit I have. According to prison rules, I can't wear leggings, skinny jeans, or yoga pants (e.g., my standard wardrobe). I settle on a pair of jeans and a loose-fitting, modest blouse.

The drive is a picturesque three hours through the Lehigh Valley and the Poconos. As we drive up the prison access road, the girls fire off one question after another.

When we walk inside, we are immediately directed to fill out a visitor form and an Ebola questionnaire.

I need to make three trips back to my car. One to put my keys away, another to put the rest of my keys away (as I misunderstood the guard the first time when he said car "key" only), and the last time to put away my watch, which I learned was also not allowed. We are only allowed to walk in with our plastic baggie of quarters and one-dollar bills for the vending machines. We then proceed through a metal detector and wait for the visitors behind us to be processed through so we can walk as a group to the visiting area.

With our hands stamped, we follow the guard in a single file line through a courtyard and into a checkpoint where our stamps are checked with a black light. We proceed through the doors into the visiting room where our hand stamps are checked yet again. I thought we'd see Matt right away, but he wasn't there yet.

The room is a large square with about twenty rectangle tables and plastic chairs arranged in configurations of four. Inmates are sitting with family members, quietly talking and keeping to themselves. A mix of raw sadness and sweet sorrow hang in the air, punctuated by moments of seeming normalcy as visitors walk to and from the vending area and the microwave, or as family members hug or play cards.

We watch a son help his elderly father into his chair. Both the father and son are clothed in the prison-issued khaki shirt and pants. Ava asks me why an old man would be in prison. What could he possibly have done wrong? I tell her that maybe he was Daddy's age when he came in and was given a very long sentence.

Prisoners are not allowed to get up from their chairs, and visitors are not allowed to stand up except to go to the bathroom or vending area. We're also instructed not to talk with anyone but our own family. About fifteen minutes after we arrive, a yellow light flashes above a door across the room. Thirty seconds later, Matt tentatively walks through the door while looking up at the guard station. The girls run over, I follow them, and we all start hugging and crying. Matt looks dehumanized in his prison uniform and black orthopedic shoes. But he is still our same Matt Daddy, and we are overjoyed to see him.

After our crying subsides, we make our way to a small table surrounded by four chairs. The first few minutes are awkward. It is hard to see my husband in a prison uniform. The girls are talking a mile a minute. They want to know everything. "What did you eat for lunch? Are your roommates here? What do you do everyday? Did you get our mail? What time do you go to bed? Why is there an old man in here? What could an old man have done wrong? Do you have money to buy things in the store?"

Matt describes everything to us. How the prisoners call each other "the guys" and the guards are called "the cops." How there is a thriving barter system and black market. The currency they use is fish! Bagged, whole, tiny mackerel in oil. We can't get over this fact and laugh hysterically at the mention of fish.

So far Matt has bartered for a pillow and for one of the guys to take his laundry bag down to the washroom every Monday morning at 6 a.m. He was able to purchase the fish with the one hundred dollars I send monthly via a Western Union account, which is the limit each prisoner is allowed to receive. Most inmates don't get that much. Their families struggle to put cash into their commissary accounts. They often go without basic items like soap, toothpaste, stamps, paper, undershirts, and socks.

Upon arrival at Allenwood, incoming inmates are issued a pair of loose-fitting khaki pants, a short-sleeved khaki shirt, shoes, a coat, a pair of grey sweat pants, a white undershirt, and a basic starter kit of travel-sized toiletries. They must purchase everything else, including phone time. The prison system relies on the commissary as a source of revenue.

Matt is animated as he tells us about the activities he has tried. He goes to the gym and the chapel, and he's joined a football team. He likes walking on the outdoor track when the weather is nice. He also goes to the library every day to write letters. Yesterday he received nine, and he replied to each one. The mailman asked him if it was his birthday. He explains how he has been trying to get into a ping-pong game, but the players won't let him. Matt is the newcomer, and the political, racial, and socially-driven cliques are strictly adhered to in prison. I told him he should just keep showing up, and eventually they might include him. I ask him about the music room, as I read there is a very good one at his facility. He tells me that is where the child molesters hang out. I want to cry.

He describes the food as "pretty good" and is surprised there is a baker who makes decent corn bread and cake. I don't imagine the food is that good, but he did say "better than airplane food." Luckily my husband happens to quite enjoy airplane food. He tells us about his two Mexican roommates, who are in prison for drug-related charges. One does not speak English. Both of them are, in his words, "quiet as church mice."

Besides Ava repeatedly asking me every five minutes during our first night if I thought Daddy was happy, I'd say our first weekend visiting Matt went really well. We saw him three days in a row and stayed two nights in the Comfort Suites by Bucknell University. The three of us were able to go out to dinner and walk around the college town and decompress after our visits. There was a lot for us to process that first weekend. But I felt strong. I felt like

I had to put on my warrior costume and protect myself and my babies as we went into battle. I was worn to the bone after that weekend, and it took me an entire week to recover.

I am my husband's keeper. Or at least I was supposed to be. I don't think I tried hard enough to help curb Matt's dysfunctional relationship with money and power. I didn't have to shop at Neiman Marcus or want a home in Nantucket. I didn't have to love traveling to exotic places or fall in love with private school education. I didn't have to use expensive skin care products and shop for organic groceries at Whole Foods. I didn't have to move from our cute 1950s colonial brick starter home in Glenside to our custom home in Wyndmoor in the name of more space, a large yard, and a pool. I feel like a walking contradiction.

I spoke to my sister Kim tonight. She calls a lot. She is concerned about my well-being. I can share with her openly, which is not typically easy for me. I am blessed to have this close relationship with her. She is a constant source of encouragement and support. Lately though, I have noticed a subtle shift.

What she doesn't explicitly say, but what I know she is thinking, lingers uncomfortably. It is the elephant in almost every room that I enter. She asks why I haven't been completely honest with my feelings about Matt.

I am protective of him and our family. And I am not ready. My loyalty is strong. Although I can write about it, I am not ready to talk about it.

I expect everyone is wondering things like, "Is Matt guilty? Do I think he is guilty? Does Matt believe he's guilty?" As my friend Iris said, "No one ends up in prison if they didn't do anything." It is hard to hear.

My mom came to Philadelphia to stay with us for a few days. Both of my parents are amazing that way. Always wanting to spend time with us and lend a helping hand. My mom and I were enjoying a quiet moment having sushi for lunch, while the girls were in school.

"Matt was doing the same thing years ago when he worked with your uncle." Her words startle me. By "the same thing," I suppose she's implying Matt was scamming people out of a fee with no intention to work the deal, or at a minimum, he was not ultimately delivering.

I am stunned. I have no idea what is real anymore. What is his truth? What is our truth? While not everyone has been as forthright in sharing their perspective, I see it in their eyes.

Do I think my husband is guilty? This seemingly straightforward question hasn't been easy for me to answer. Matt convinces me over and over that he did nothing illegal. I want to believe that. Ethical matters are a different story.

Early in his career, when he first started working for Arlen, Matt was handed deals that seemed unlikely to close. Working class customers in search of the American Dream came to Matt's company seeking $25,000 – $100,000 in investor money to start their dream businesses. And they'd invest their $5,000 or $10,000 of life savings to pay the firm's non-refundable fee to find investors, with no guarantees.

Sometimes Matt would ask my opinion of a deal. So many of them seemed paper-thin to me. When I'd plead with him not to take the fee, he'd shut me down. "These people believe in their businesses, and if they don't come to me, Jenn, they will go to someone else, so why shouldn't I be the one to work the deal?"

"But aren't you unlikely to find an investor? That will leave them high and dry."

I eventually tuned out his rationalizing, and he stopped asking my opinion. I believe that Matt's intentions were sincere in the beginning. I believe that he was often handed deals that were almost impossible to find funding for, but he worked on them because it was his job. Even a remote chance to make money seemed to challenge and excite him.

I may never know when or how he was made aware of the scheme. Whenever I confront him, he unwaveringly replies, "I always worked the deals. I actually closed some that everyone said were impossible! I was not out to scam anyone. I knew the odds were often one in a hundred—that for every hundred deals I took, I would only be able to close one. This is the nature of the business, Jenn." I believed him.

Even as I wrestle with my feelings about my husband's culpability, I want to shield my girls from the details as long as I can. They haven't raised the question of Matt's guilt in a long time. In the beginning, when they'd ask question after question about the wrongdoings Matt was accused of, I'd answer them as honestly but as gingerly as I could. I told them what I believed at the time. I told them that his old company was in trouble with the law for stealing money but that Daddy was wrongly accused. I believed this to be true. I also explained the trial process to them, and told them we made a mistake by not working with the judge and saying sorry in the beginning.

I am not sure how I will respond when the topic of his guilt reemerges. The girls can handle a lot. I will try my very best to prevent the dysfunction of my husband's choices from causing them harm. I am trying not to overprotect them. They ask so many questions, and sometimes I sugarcoat the answers. I need to be honest, but I also need to not overwhelm them. It's a fine line, and often my need for truth causes me to blur the line more often than I care to admit.

CHAPTER FIFTEEN

Inside

January 2015

Being locked up with hundreds of other men, many who come from extreme poverty, has not only humbled my husband, it may have saved his life. With no access to making money or using drugs or alcohol, and nothing else to do besides look inside himself, reflect upon his choices, exercise, and read, Matt has a new thirteen-year plan. May he use it well.

Other than missing us like crazy, Matt is quickly adjusting to and even appreciating the simplicity of his new life. He talks honestly about the quiet, the lack of stress, and even his relief at having no responsibilities. Perhaps this is a bizarre honeymoon stage, and sometime soon the reality of what he is missing on the outside will surpass the contentment he feels on the inside.

My husband talks with wonderment about having the space and time to think. Prior to his incarceration, he didn't allow himself these luxuries. The "old" Matt would not have respected the man who didn't work an eighty-hour week. I am glad he is experiencing the benefits of time and space and centering. Of course, I wish the cost of this lesson wasn't imprisonment. But perhaps this is part of God's plan for Matt.

Matt's entire perspective on life is being challenged now that he is living on equal ground with an ethnically diverse population of criminals. Many of "the guys" have not completed high school. They are convicted drug addicts, drug dealers, and sex offenders. They survived the hood by becoming involved in gangs and thievery. Matt's two roommates are from the Mexican Mafia. One of his new friends is part of the Colombo family. The "kids" he tutors are typically in for using or selling heroin. The people Matt used to refer to as the dregs of society are now his peers.

On our next visit to Allenwood, it is just me and Ava because Eliza is performing in a dance competition. Matt tells us he is finding some peace and comfort in the ease of his routine and the manageability of what is expected of him. He likes his job, which is a two-hour shift, five times a week monitoring gym equipment and straightening up the weights. He seems to be adjusting well. I am somewhat relieved.

Matt promises to call us that night to make sure we arrived home safely, but we don't receive the expected phone call. On the third night after our visit, the girls and I are in the kitchen doing homework and making dinner when Matt calls. "You have a pre-paid call from a federal prison, if you want to accept the charges dial five now." He is on speaker, and the girls are chattering to him about their day.

A minute into the call, he asks to speak with me privately. I know something is very wrong. I go into my office and shut the door. Matt's voice shakes as he tells me he is in solitary confinement. The SHU. Solitary Housing Unit. The Hole. I hear myself screaming, "No, no, no! Oh please, I can't take this." Matt starts crying while telling me he is okay. He's in an 8' x 10' foot room with a cot and a toilet. He is receiving meals through a slot at the bottom of the door. He has a book. Nothing else.

Then he tells me why he was put in solitary confinement. Apparently, when Ava and I left Sunday afternoon, Matt was strip-searched. He said this is procedure after leaving the visiting room. Matt had been playing football the previous Friday night. He is not in the best shape and is much older than the other inmates, but he is strong and fast and they like him. That night their kicker was not available so they asked him to stand in. Against his better judgment, he did. He pulled his hamstring on the first kick.

When he was strip-searched, the guards saw the bruise on his leg and asked how he got it. When he said it was from playing football, they asked him if he went to medical. He told them he was fine and didn't think he needed to go. They didn't like that answer. They sent him to get his bruise checked. There they asked him if he got into a fight. He said no. They said that they would have to "investigate" this and threw him in the Hole. They told him he'd be allowed one phone call in thirty days, which he used on day three to call me.

The girls run into the office when they hear me crying. They start crying too. After we cry and hug each other for a while and I assure them Daddy is safe, we solemnly return to homework.

I can no longer sleep. Years of good sleep habits left me when Matt did. I woke up tonight after just three hours, my heart beating fast and my body slick with sweat. I had a nightmare about Matt. I was visiting him in prison but could not physically reach him. He was suffering. I was scared. Authority figures dominated. Other details escape me. All I know is that my heart is in my throat.

It's day eleven of Matt's solitary confinement. I just missed a call from "No Caller ID." I am sick with worry it may have been Matt. Is it possible he has been released from the SHU and is feeling desperate to reconnect? My gut tells me it was not him, but I wait by the phone shaking with worry and anticipation.

Matt's parents left yesterday. They visited us for five days. Their stoicism is simultaneously admirable and infuriating. I can only imagine that their less-than-emotional approach to everything is purely a defense mechanism. A crutch they rely on to get through each day.

During their visit, I shared with them many of my recent revelations and findings. As I was going through boxes and boxes of paperwork, I came to realize that Matt has been embroiled in one legal mess after another for nearly a decade. I had no idea how extensive and pervasive his legal problems were. Again I feel betrayed. Why did he not share more of the details of what he was going through? Did he not trust me? Was he afraid I would leave him? Was he ashamed? Worried about disappointing me?

I tried to be as gentle as possible as I explained to Matt's parents the details of the financial mess Matt left me in. I also told Matt's mother about his long pattern of dishonesty and covering up wrongdoings. I told her about several other lawsuits that Matt has been mired in for years, which are unrelated to the charges that landed him in prison.

Matt's mom was defensive at first, then she began asking me for the specifics. She sat and listened to what I had to say. I told her how Matt always pretended that everything was under control. That he would never acknowledge his transgressions. Ever. I think he believed that everything would be okay. In fact, I bet he is sitting in solitary confinement as I sit at home writing these words, fully confident he will endure. Perhaps this is how he chooses to protect himself from pain. If nothing else, this is how Matt survives his life.

I wanted Matt's parents and in particular his mom to say, "My son was wrong for the things he did. Your feelings are valid. His actions have hurt you and many other people!" When I showed his parents the delinquent bills and letters from lawyers strewn across my makeshift desk (the dining room table), their response was simply, "It looks like you have it all under control." This is how it is. I try not to judge them for how they choose to deal with their pain because at the end of the day we are all just trying to survive.

Matt called me yesterday (day fifteen) to tell me he was finally out of the SHU. His first words were, "I made it, Jenny." I nearly collapsed in relief. Matt went on to explain that although the investigation confirmed there was no fight, he was subsequently left in confinement because the only person who could release him had gone on vacation for two weeks the day after Matt was put in the SHU.

For the next forty-eight hours, I actually experienced something that resembled happiness. Our weekend plans changed. The girls and I are going to visit their Daddy on Valentine's Day.

CHAPTER SIXTEEN

Our New Normal

February 2015

As I walk into Allenwood on Valentine's Day, something inside me shifts. My head is down, I am wearing a long black skirt, and I make eye contact with no one. When Matt was in the SHU, I was put in touch with a woman named Ivy, who had served a long prison sentence in Connecticut for a crime similar to Matt's. Now Ivy volunteers at the Rikers Island Prison Complex. She teaches yoga to inmates and provides moral support and advice for prisoners' spouses. She was nothing less than a godsend.

Ivy told me about the harrowing twenty-seven days she endured in solitary confinement upon arrival at a federal prison in New England. Drawing from some of her experiences, I managed to create a story about Matt's SHU stint that greatly affected my mood that visit. I convinced myself I had been too friendly with the guards before, and that Matt was punished with solitary confinement to bring him down a notch because he seemed too happy, as did his wife and daughters.

Not wanting to draw attention to myself or my family, I am quiet and withdrawn. I feel depressed, defeated, and exhausted. This is the seventh time I am walking into this horrible place in less than six weeks. Upon entering the crowded visiting room, I am assaulted by the stench of the vending machine chicken and other unsavory items purchased with quarters then microwaved and served up on tiny paper plates. Trash is strewn across every table, from discarded imitation Twinkie wrappers to half-eaten packages of chicken wings. I am unable to access a shred of peace or even a fake smile.

The visit is rocky from the start. Matt tears up when he starts asking Eliza about her upcoming gymnastics competition. I feel intensely resentful. How does he have a right to be sad? This was so preventable. Wasn't it? He missed out on so much when they were younger, and now he will miss everything until they are adults.

Matt then begins talking about "his business" and asks the girls if people still call his BlackBerry. Really? What the fuck??!! I dig my nails into my skin and excuse myself to go to the bathroom. When I return, he proceeds to tell me about an idea for he and I to go into business together when he gets out of prison. What??!! I wouldn't go into business with him if my life depended on it.

He presses me to tell him what's going on for me. I start to, but it is difficult to speak for more than a minute or two before the girls get bored and interrupt. And of course we are censoring ourselves for their benefit. But because it is very loud in the visiting room, we sneak in a few choice words here and there until I can't hold back anymore. I tell him I am angry with him and furious he hurt so many people. I tell him my family is also angry with him, that he and Jackie were a destructive team, and his attempts to protect me by covering up the truth destroyed us.

I tell him he's lost everything, and he still is not taking any responsibility for his actions. That while he keeps trying to blame his lawyer, the pressure to provide for and raise our girls is mine alone. I am the one who suffers the most.

He says he wants to strategize with me on how he can help. He says he is sorry I am hurting, yet he still doesn't assume any sense of ownership for his mistakes. Does it even matter at this point? He's ruined his own life and done irreparable damage to his family.

How do I keep focused on the present when I am so angry about the past? How do I not worry about the future? How do I keep from ruminating? I try to create healthy distractions and take care of myself, but I continually find myself back in "need of repair" mode. I do what needs to be done for a few hours, then, exhausted, I crawl back into bed. Sleep is the only place I find true peace.

I was planning to take the girls to visit Matt again next weekend, but I just can't do it. Instead, my parents will visit him for the first time, and the girls and I will go the following weekend. Maybe every other week is too ambitious. I am burnt out. My self-imposed pressure to help ease Matt's suffering and make sure the girls frequently see their father is wearing me down.

The girls sense this. Eliza asks me if I still love Daddy. They both know I am unhappy. Ava has started to overplay her happy or silly moments to try to make me laugh and keep things light. Eliza asks me why I can't be happy like I was before. I try to explain that sometimes that is not possible, and my happiness is not her or her sister's responsibility.

The recurring theme that comes up with my friends is, "You need to start to move on with your life." While I don't disagree, I don't know what to do differently. Despite my anger at his actions, I can't eradicate my sense of responsibility to my husband. I feel it's my job to foster the girls' relationship with their father. More often than I'd like to admit, I find myself mired in a heap of resentment.

As I write this, Eliza is sitting next to me texting her gymnastics coach about her father being in prison. Earlier this evening, she told me she was thinking about telling her coach, and I encouraged her to do so. Somehow Eliza's text exchange with her coach pops up on my computer, and I see their online conversation unfold. Witnessing Eliza's raw honest sharing, coupled with the vulnerability she reveals to her coach by text, makes me cry. I turn my head away so Eliza doesn't see the tears.

Lately, Eliza has been preoccupied with ritualistic eating habits. She carefully regulates herself with a controlled and often restrictive diet. Meticulously planning her daily meals, ever so careful not to exceed one dessert while making sure she has enough protein and vegetables. She's constantly on the Internet, searching for nutrition advice. In health class last semester, she learned about diet, calories, food content, and body image. I am concerned Eliza will take these new habits too far. I watch closely and try not to make it worse by challenging her.

Eliza has always had an obsessive nature. However, this obsession feels different, and it concerns me. Her life has been turned upside down. Her father leaving for prison is just the first of many changes she will have to endure over the next few years. I understand her desire to control her life, but I never expected this. I grew up watching my mother struggle with an eating disorder, then my sister.

I purposely don't talk about calories or weight or good food versus bad food. I strive to serve nurturing food and make the dinner table a happy place. There is always dessert. I want their experience of eating to be healthy and enjoyable.

My girls aren't the only ones suffering. My father tells me that dealing with Matt's fallout is making him sick, actually physically ill. He is not sure he can stomach going up to see Matt this weekend. I encourage my dad to go if he feels like he might be up to it, and to be honest with Matt about the damage his actions have caused. My father is hesitant about confronting Matt, afraid that he will hurt him while he is vulnerable. I tell my dad we are all enabling Matt when we don't tell him how we feel.

Not that Matt will be ready to hear any of it. Judging by his letters and how he responds to me when I share how badly he fucked up, Matt is still nowhere close to taking responsibility. To the contrary, he accuses me of villainizing him.

My heart goes out to my father. He has been tirelessly handling the bulk of the cleanup from Matt's messes. My father has been the one talking to all the lawyers, accountants, business partners, and clients. He is doing this for me because I can't.

I used to think Matt possessed the gift of making the impossible possible. In the beginning of his career, I admired his business style. He was persistent, smart, and witty, and he could sell anything. As I matured and my perspective changed, qualities that used to attract me began to repel me. His business style became aggressive, argumentative, and conniving. He had a growing need to debate, to be right, and to win. His shrewd approach to deal-making won him many awards and prestige. Often I was proud of his accomplishments. But increasingly I became wary of his methodology and of his lack of empathy.

On our frequent road trips to Nantucket or DC or Maine, sitting in the passenger seat, I'd be appalled at the volatility of his work-related conversations, especially during deal closings. He would shrug off my reaction, saying, "This is just business, Jenn." I didn't agree, nor did I like the toxicity of these business exchanges. He earned a reputation as a shark and was proud of it.

While I continued to outwardly support him, little by little I was beginning to lose respect for him. As his wife, this feels horrible to admit, but it's true. It pains me to know he will read this someday. He thought that I was ever critical of him. Maybe I was, but I did continue to love and support him. I knew the other side of him. I knew and loved the Matt who helped me so much in the beginning of our relationship. The Matt who grounded me and modeled kindness, light, and love. He loved me well for so long. Until he didn't.

When among friends and family, Matt was brilliant, charming, fun, and funny. My parents, sisters, and their spouses were Matt's biggest fans. I was seen as the difficult one, while Matt was looked upon as golden. I was the one who was too rigid. When I tried to set limits on his smoking or drinking, I might hear, "Oh you are so prudish. Let boys be boys."

Matt felt he was invincible. And he loved the rush of risk. As my father once commented, "Matt skates around the edges." This is how he chose to live his life. Taking risks was his mantra. One of the first items he purchased when we moved to Philadelphia was a huge framed poster with "RISK" written in large letters and a cheesy slogan about what it means to take risks in life.

Never in a million years did I think his risk taking would lead to the destruction of his family, not to mention many other people's dreams, and the end of his freedom. Although my therapist has pointed out that I was attracted to Matt in part because of this very same characteristic, ultimately his risk taking became one of the greatest strains in our marriage. It has left us where we are today. Fulfilling my darkest fantasy of being alone and abandoned.

Monday morning the shit hits the fan. I can't deal. My dad reaches his boiling point. The second mortgage that was taken out on our Wyndmoor home is coming up for renewal. My father is done. He wrote Matt a letter, which he also sent to me and to Matt's parents. My dad has taken on too much of the burden, and he no longer wants to be in charge of cleanup duty. I understand, and I am deeply grateful he has done this much. But I am starting to fall apart again.

Have the past twenty years of my life been a lie? I find myself getting lost in the pictures on our walls. The ethereal wedding portraits with us barefoot in the sand. The handsome family photo in the backyard when the girls were five and seven. I am holding Ava, and Eliza grins wide as she leans into Matt. The angelic black-and-white baby pictures of Eliza with a strand of pearls around her neck, and the photos of Ava sitting bare-bottomed on a fur rug. I distinctly remember each photo session and am pained by these images of happiness long gone.

The luxuries we enjoyed and the life we lived suddenly feel like a dream. But my current life also feels unreal. What is true?

I blame myself. How could I let this happen? I always thought Matt handled our finances so well. He was so savvy, so organized. How could I have been so off? Or, was I? We were well prepared for the future until recently when our million dollars in savings was depleted to pay lawyers to defend Matt. The girls and I are now penniless.

As I unearth the details of the unethical nature of Matt's business and financial practices, the damage he wrought on hundreds of victims as well as those closest to him is staggering. It makes me nauseous to consider that someday the girls will know the truth.

When we originally told the girls that Matt was completely innocent, I believed it. Now I feel duplicitous. I wrestle with when and how to have these important conversations with Eliza and Ava. How will they reconcile what they discover with the sweet, funny, playful Daddy they love and adore?

I decide that for now the vision they have of their father need not nor should not match mine. They have many years ahead of them to draw their own conclusions about Matt, just as I'm trying to do now.

Another topic that hasn't yet entered the girls' world—it would be premature at the moment—is whether their parents will divorce. It is a possibility I couldn't even fathom until recently.

Each time I pack up to go visit Matt, I convince myself this is my wifely duty. I made a vow to stand by him for better or for worse. Yet each prison visit stirs up more pain to process when I get home. Prison visit equals emotional tailspin. The recovery time is brutal. This is our new normal, and it sucks.

No one moves through life unchanged. We are all damaged. I am not the same person I was when Matt first met me, nor is he the same man I fell in love with. Life has me wanting more intimacy and spirituality, and life has beaten Matt down in ways I will never fully understand.

I am only now beginning to fully grasp the extent to which Matt consistently evades the truth. I used to think it was just his way of trying to spin a good story, but as I look back, I see he was always trying to impress. Soon after we met, he told me his family owned a home in Vermont. They didn't. Most of his lies stemmed from insecurity or a desire to please. I considered them to be benign. That was when I believed there was such a thing as an inconsequential, little white lie. Later on he would tell me things I wanted to hear, and I hungered to believe everything he said to me. I wanted and needed him to be someone he was not.

I am indignant about the debt Matt has encumbered me with, and angrier still about his lack of remorse. When I talk to him on the phone or in letters about being shocked and overwhelmed by the financial mess, he completely downplays it. When I press him, when I push for accountability, he challenges me. He asks me why I insist he admit to his specific wrongdoings. "Why do you need this from me, Jenn?" No matter my reply, he offers nothing more.

That Matt seems incapable of recognizing and acknowledging his mistakes leads me to seriously wonder, "Is he is a sociopath? Did I marry a sociopath? Is the father of my children a sociopath?" And if so, how do I process this information?

I know I must accept that I can't change Matt. He has a fierce grip on his perspective, and his experience is his own. I seem to have very little influence on what he thinks and does. Challenging and questioning his behavior only adds fuel to his fire. Do we even have a marriage anymore?

When Matt was in solitary confinement, everyone was devastated. We pulled together and prayed for him. My worry was softened only because my family shared my pain and grief. As new information continues to emerge about second mortgages I didn't know about, delinquent car payments, lingering lawsuits, monies owed to accountants and lawyers, and as I peel back layers of longstanding deceptions, we are all reeling. At times I feel distant from my family, as we take turns pulling away and withdrawing to personally process the mounting evidence of Matt's dishonesty and betrayal.

CHAPTER SEVENTEEN

Out with the Old, In with the New

Spring 2015

When Matt had been gone for three months, when spring was starting to provide me with renewed energy, and when I could finally walk over to the office and garage without crying, I knew it was time to get to work.

Cleaning out Matt's home office was cathartic. The first step was getting his huge, expensive entertainment system out and into a consignment shop. Then, one by one, I tackled the framed pictures and abundant knick-knacks that went into one of three piles: save, trash, or garage sale.

I ended up selling much of it on eBay and Facebook. My financial situation left little room for sentiment. The only item I initially was reluctant to sell was the large framed photograph of the San Juan Mountains I had given to Matt for our tenth wedding anniversary. But I relented, and with some remorse and a dash of spite, I earned enough from that Mangelsen photo for a month's worth of groceries.

I also discovered the joy of the barter system. Much-needed massages and technical support were exchanged for lamps, furniture, and computers. When I aggressively threw Matt's marijuana paraphernalia into the trash, I enjoyed the shattering of a purple glass bong. The few items I saved for him are housed in a corner of the garage.

For several weeks, the office looked clean, fresh, and simple. Then the remainder of the furniture sold. Two of my neighbors bought most of it, and I moved several pieces into the house. Now the office was completely empty, stripped down, and ugly. Matt would have been devastated to see it in this state. For many years, this was his haven, the space he designed, built, and adorned with pride.

Purging his office was necessary not only for the emotional cleansing and release it provided, but also to make room for the yoga studio I hope will help support us. The idea to turn Matt's office into a yoga studio arose before Matt left. It began as a way to help the girls focus on something fun. They are both dancers, so at first we talked about creating a dance studio.

Ava wanted to pick out the paint colors and suggested a mirror on one wall and a couch and furry rug for a lounge area. None of that happened. I decided there would be no exchange of money for this project. Here's what did happen. I advertised on Facebook, "Labor needed in exchange for Matt's motorcycle." My friend Lisa immediately responded and put me in touch with her two cousins from South Philly.

Eager to leave with Matt's motorcycle, it took them just four days to pull out the carpet and replace it with bamboo flooring. I placed a few needed pieces of furniture back into the space, set up a small stereo, then brought in yoga mats, blankets, crystals, incense, and candles. That was it. The girls were disappointed they couldn't have their mirror, but we all enjoy the fresh, serene space we created.

Thus the Wyndmoor Studio was born in May, five months after Matt went to prison. It was a symbolic and a physical transformation. The studio is a beautiful place filled with positive energy and love. As the sun streams in through the French doors that open onto the deck, it feels like peace. It feels like hope. It feels like home. I hired a yoga instructor and began holding classes. I also leased the space to a massage therapist and began selling my mala beads. I am proud of the studio. The necessary conversion of what used to be a source of pain has become a beacon of light.

This morning on our drive to school, Ava began telling me about the $400,000 Lamborghini that Nicki Minaj bought and that she wished she, too, could be famous and rich. When I responded with the lamest cliché, "Well you know money doesn't make you happy," she was quick to reply, "Well it can depending on how you use it."

Then out of her mouth came, "How is Daddy going to pay back the $26 million?" What??? I really didn't know what she meant for a second. When I asked her what she was talking about, she told me one of her friends at school said, "My mom tells me everything, and your dad knew what he was doing when he took money from all those people." I was speechless.

Ava went on to explain that she told her friend she was wrong. While I tried to appear neutral and unemotional, Ava sensed my concern. She assured me it was "no big deal" that she and this friend Googled Matt during free time at school, which is when she read about the retribution. WTF??!! I told her that she is not to Google Daddy at school, but that she and I could Google him together if she wanted to learn more about what was written in the papers. I told her how sorry I was that she had to deal with this. She then asked me why I told my friend Poppy about Daddy, especially since she is such a new friend. I told her that Poppy is a friend from my yoga retreat, and that everyone shared really sad stuff there.

Ava wanted to know more about the retreat. I briefly told her about a suicide and a sexual abuse victim. God help me. It is no surprise that Ava has made a permanent move to my bed. My goal was not only to deflect our own painful family problems, but also to show her that other families also face difficult challenges. I am devastated that my baby, my ten-year-old, is hearing this at such a tender age.

Yesterday afternoon I experienced a total blood sugar drop and had to lie down for about thirty minutes until it passed. I had the chills and felt faint and nauseous. When dinnertime came and went without my moving and Eliza came upstairs to ask me to make her pasta, I told her she would have to make it on her own. She did.

In Matt's absence, Eliza has adopted a quality of independence that surprises and impresses me. Her self-awareness and interpretation of the needs of our new family dynamic is reflected in her increased helpfulness around the house. Knowing that she is able make dinner, do laundry, arrange her social agenda, take care of her body, and work hard at school and sports is an immense help to me.

That being said, the rising and falling moods in this all-female household can be intense. Ava's highs and lows are those of a typical preteen. She is happiest when friends are over, relishing in the play and laughter that allows her to be a kid. When playtime ends, she often finds comfort and temporary distraction by eating snacks in front of the television.

Invariably when I ask her to do something she perceives as work, she behaves as if she's just been presented with an insurmountable hardship. She whines and delivers an almost toddler-like "NO!" Homework, bedtime, cleaning up after herself, playing with the dog, getting dressed, and HAIR. Each one of her usual responsibilities has turned into a battle.

Lately she blames me for every ounce of her unhappiness. Well-established habits have regressed to early childhood behaviors. She refuses to talk about Matt. I took the girls to a therapist a few times each, and they viewed it as a punishment. In the past when Ava misbehaved, she'd return to me minutes later with a sincere heartfelt apology. Ever since Matt left, her outbursts are more frequent and apologies are nonexistent.

Everything is changing so fast. My family life, my social life, my entire life as I knew it. I don't think anyone knows what to do with me. Recently I was not invited to a friend's birthday party. It was a surprise sixtieth. I am sure if Matt were here, we would have been invited.

I get the sense people are not comfortable with me. I am single, but not really. My husband is in prison. This is a threat. Why? Does being around me trigger guilt or fear? Guilt that they haven't written Matt? Fear that our situation is contagious? Discomfort that the wife of a criminal might contaminate their parties? Will inviting me to their parties make them look bad or otherwise harm their social standing? Do they fear I'll go after their husbands? I don't know. In any event, my feelings were extremely hurt.

Even when others don't exclude me or treat me differently, I can't help feeling different. Tonight there was a "Montgomery Gals" gathering—a get together with women in my neighborhood. In fact, it is a monthly tradition I initiated six years ago, in my neighborhood, on our street, Montgomery Avenue. Our monthly gatherings tend to be fun and lighthearted, and they have helped bring us together as women, neighbors, and friends.

Everyone is genuinely concerned about my well-being. When they ask how the girls and I are doing and how Matt is adjusting to prison, I answer them honestly. I wonder if being honest is too hard for most people? I feel like I bring people down, that we come together for release, not to go on about our misery. I wonder if I will ever have happier answers to their questions.

In the six months since Matt was incarcerated, my perspective has changed dramatically. My world feels different and strange. How will I feel in another six months? In the relatively short time we have been apart, I have learned how to do tasks I had never done. Selling a house, online banking, taxes. I can now put the bike rack on the car and fix the toilet when it runs.

More important than the day-to-day tasks, I am learning how to be alone. How to be single. How to not be paired. How to be lonely. As time goes on, I am finding my way. Forging a new road, one without a husband, one without Matt.

I never expected to be a single parent. I thought about how hard it must be when I saw a few of my friends do it. I assumed I wouldn't be able to handle it. But here I am, and now my only hope is that I take on the challenge with grace. I like the independence but not the instability of my circumstances.

Matt's phone calls and letters are helpful to the girls. Their connection with their father is important, and I will help them maintain a relationship with him. But my connection to Matt has weakened. I am pulling away. Perhaps in equal parts self-preservation, anger, and sadness.

I see couples in the visiting area that seem to be smoothly navigating their prison relationship. I wish I knew how they do it. The other day I noticed a man who was in solitary confinement having his visit through the glass, and he was smiling. His wife held up her hand to the glass and his joined hers. I was actually jealous of them.

Matt and I haven't shared that kind of love and intimacy in years. There were obstacles before, and now this one. The statistics I read are not particularly hopeful either. Most couples end their marriage either after or during an incarceration, especially when the prison sentence is greater than five years.

My obsession to get visitors up to Allenwood also has ceased. I was making myself sick up until the beginning of May trying to get the SignUpGenius spots filled so Matt had visitors every weekend. I can't do it anymore. As soon as I stopped, the spots went largely unfilled. I assume it will continue that way. One exception is Matt's friend Henrick who signed up again on his own initiative. I appreciate that more than he probably knows. The other exceptions are Matt's parents, who are quite loyal and continue visiting him every six weeks or so.

Yesterday was our nineteenth wedding anniversary. I came home from errands to find a large, gorgeous floral arrangement from Robertson's sitting on my doorstep. White and yellow orchids, roses, and hydrangeas. The card confirmed they were from Matt. The tears and sadness I have repressed in recent weeks came pouring out. The card was beautiful and spoke of much happier times.

CHAPTER EIGHTEEN
Return to Boulder

Summer 2015

The girls go to camp, and I go to Boulder. I feel like I'm home the moment I get off the plane. Breathtaking views of the Rockies immediately invigorate me. The thin mountain air, bright sun, puffy white clouds, and brilliant blue sky bring me close to something earthy and benevolent.

Colorado's familiarity comforts and softens me. I am relaxed and alert. I feel blessed. I am reunited with my soul. Summer in the mountains feels like my birthright. It greets me like an old friend, wrapping its beauty around me.

Returning to Boulder stirs up feelings of possibility and hope, desire and longing. As I walk around town, I can't stop smiling. I feel like I did in 1986 when I arrived at the University of Colorado as a freshman, just shy of my eighteenth birthday. I was wanting for nothing and hoping for everything. Excited and free, believing that *this* is exactly what true happiness feels like.

My parents had flown out with me to help set up my small dorm room with its tall window overlooking Farrand Field. They took me to Target and McGuckin Hardware, where we purchased eighties decor and my version of teenage essentials including a Cure poster, a hot plate, and a set of pastel sheets in hues of mint green, lavender, and mauve.

I originally was introduced to Boulder when I was fourteen while on a six-week teen tour of the western states, where we camped in national parks and stayed in college dorms. Immediately smitten with this Rocky Mountain enclave, I knew I would return. The first time was three years later to attend the University of Colorado, and here I am again now, twenty-five years after graduating. I am hungry to take it all in—meet new people, see old friends, and revisit my past. Euphoria and nostalgia wash over me.

As I walk through the halls of the UMC, then along the leafy streets where I lived off campus, I am flooded with memories and adrenaline. The Flatirons stand tall and protective behind me as I stroll through my old neighborhoods looking for the places I used to live. My sophomore year, it was on Marine Street with Sandy and Bucky. When I find the run-down cluster of one-story apartments I used to call home, I can't help but stare. I flash back to my small bedroom, which I had painted peach and decorated with white twinkle lights and gypsy scarves. Down the street, I recognize the cute blue house with the wraparound porch where Melissa, Karen, and Tommy lived and late-night parties were frequent and uninhibited.

I walk a few blocks to The Hill. It is remarkably as I remember it. The Fox Theater, which used to be called Tulagi, still has a prominent marquee boasting the current show. This was the venue where I fell in love with the Boulder bands Big Head Todd and The Monsters, Leftover Salmon, and The Samples. We drank horrible libations like 3.2 beer and shots of Jägermeister while crowding close to the stage and dancing all night.

Then I visit the tan house on 18th, where I lived with Jenny, Amy, and Tom. I loved its outdoor hot tub, picket fence, and that the Boulder Creek flowed behind it. The house was brand new when I rented it. In fact, it was under construction when I first walked in and asked to speak to the owner. More than two decades later, it is old, ugly, and in disrepair. It was sad to see in this state. Taking it in, I contemplated the power of time and memory, before walking away with a small lump in my heart.

Strolling down Pearl Street, I notice fancy new stores mixed in with stores I remember like Peppercorn and The

Trident Bookstore. Bittersweetness courses like a drug through my veins as I remember love lost and youth gone by. Sadness bubbles up slowly then flutters away as quickly as it came. Throughout my five days in Boulder, I feel like I am being held in a physical cloud of remembrance. Auspicious and precarious, I feel as if I am coming and going in and out of a dream. Almost like déjà vu.

I have breakfast at the still popular Lucille's Cajun Cafe with Eric, a friend I haven't seen or spoken to in over twenty years. Housed in the same yellow Victorian since its founding thirty-two years ago, a line of patrons dutifully wait on the sidewalk to enter as soon as the doors open each morning, just like when I was at CU. Once inside, the aroma of beignets and strong coffee permeates the almost humid air in this tiny, old building with its kitchen that works overtime.

After biscuits, café au lait, and eggs Sardou, Eric and I stroll along the Boulder Creek. When we stop to sit on a rock and dip our feet into the deliciously cold snowmelt, I am in heaven. The creek is a special place for me. I used to spend a lot of time here alone, meditating in the sun, and cooling off in the water. It is one of my fondest memories of Boulder. And the sweet, creek smell! Intoxicating.

Eric and I talk about paths we have chosen in our lives so far, regrets, and desires for the future. As we watch kids float down the late summer water in inner tubes, I remember how alive I felt when exploration and adventure circulated in the air. I inhale the scent of summer.

I suddenly feel like I am falling in love again—with myself, with life, with new possibilities. It's as if I have been blessed with new eyes that are slowly being opened to what is, what was, and what will be. I barely sleep. I joke that I am suffering from pure excitement. I feel truly alive for the first time in a very long time.

I know without a doubt I want to move out West. I had an eight-year plan, based on when both girls would have finished high school, but now I can't fathom shelving this dream for that long. I hunger to be surrounded by kindred spirits in ways that I haven't experienced in Philadelphia, despite my dear friends there.

Yet I worry how a move would affect my girls. Who knows? Maybe after middle school they would welcome the change. Even if they did, there are other complications. Besides the uprooting factor, there is Matt to consider. What would it mean for us to move so far away from him? I guess he could ask to be relocated, but then what about his parents who continue to visit him regularly?

Friends and family repeatedly advise, "You need to do what is best for you." Easier said than done. To confront the myriad of challenges this kind of cross-country move would entail, I would need to want this dream more than anything in the world. In this moment, I do.

The momentum and energy I am tapping into during this short visit to Boulder are enabling me to recognize goals that until now have been loosely circling in my brain. The one I am most excited about is finding my editor, Stacey Stern. Stacey is an old friend from Potomac. Our families shared a home together in the 1970s in Bethany Beach, Delaware. I loved that house and our summers there. I hadn't seen Stacey in over thirty years, although we casually reconnected a few years ago through Facebook.

Stacey has lived in Boulder for more than twenty years, arriving in the early 1990s soon after I left. To have lunch with her so many years later, catch up on milestones in our adult lives, learn she edits books just when I decided it was time to find an editor, and now to launch our collaboration on this book feels like nothing less than "kismet," to borrow the Arabic-turned-Turkish word for fate.

CHAPTER NINETEEN

Moving On

Committing to move forward with my book—and my life—excites and scares me. I am in an in-between place of waiting for what will be while also trying to remain focused and take the necessary steps to continue my transformation. The changes seem endless, beginning of course, with the ongoing adjustment to the pain and strangeness of having my husband go off to prison for a long time.

I am starting to get used to the void. The pain has dulled to where it is bearable, although I am nowhere close to acceptance yet. When I experience joy, I am surprised and grateful. When I am depressed for days in a row, I am surprised and discouraged.

My anger has receded to what feels like a permanent resting place. Never inaccessible, it rears its ugliness both at expected and unexpected times. A typical trigger for me lately is when I hear the phone ring and the phone's speaker announce, "You have a pre-paid call from a federal prison. To accept this call dial five, to decline or block future calls from this number dial seven now."

Learning the minutia of our household finances feels like trying to run a sinking business. Bills, taxes, debt collectors, mortgages, and lawsuits.

I am pounced upon regularly and unexpectedly. My visceral reaction is fury. Unpaid taxes from Springfield Township, letters in the mail from the accountant asking for $5,000 Matt owes him, phone calls from a major television network asking for my side of the story.

Navigating my new life as a single parent is really fucking hard. I have to ask for help, which is my least favorite thing to do. It is undeniably humbling. The other day I was in bed with a debilitating migraine. I called several people in search of a ride home for Eliza from sports. It is way outside my comfort zone to be this needy. My friend Larry helped out. I was shamefully appreciative. But sometimes friends that I think might lend a hand tell me they cannot help. To reach out and have to be in a position to ask is hard enough, being turned down feels awful and embarrassing.

I am trying to figure out where I fit in socially. I have been abandoned by coupledom. I didn't realize I would be treated differently as a single person. I naively assumed friends would be more than willing to have me tag along. I thought I would continue to be invited out on weekends and to parties, but it is not happening. Since Matt was incarcerated, I have not been invited out once on a weekend. Are people that uncomfortable with me? Or with the dynamic of the third wheel? Are they afraid they will "catch" what I have, what has happened to me? Even if it's nothing personal, it hurts. And of course it is personal.

Acknowledging to myself that I want and need love, friendship, and intimacy has been a relief. But the relief is quickly followed by guilt then fear. Contemplating dating makes me feel as if I am abandoning my husband. Yet I can't deny that the prospect of dating both intrigues and terrifies me.

How can I possibly trust someone again? I feel incredibly vulnerable and unsure. Am I ready? I know I will have to be real and true and honest with myself and others—but I fear most people will not be able to handle my truth. The truth of having a husband in prison. The truth of my pain. The truth of who I am and of my deepest fears.

Sometimes I want to reach for an Ativan. I keep them hidden behind the Advil in my medicine chest. Twenty-five years with Matt, and not once did I stray. As I open my eyes and begin to learn more about being single and dating again, I am cautious, nervous, and anticipatory.

Matt and I uncomfortably discuss my dating. A few minutes on a phone call, maybe a paragraph in a letter, or briefly while sitting across from him in the visiting room at Allenwood. We approach the topic with kid gloves. He claims to be supportive. I am impressed but not surprised by his stoicism. I know he wants me to be happy, and I think it gives him a strange solace that maybe I will be looked after. He even suggested someone for me and said he wondered if I wasn't already dating this person. It's bizarre. Imagining a future with another man makes me feel strange, disconnected to who I was and who I am.

Soon after I return from my remarkable trip to Boulder, autumn approaches. I do not like this season. As the weather cools, the lightness and ease of summer days give way to structured schedules with new rhythms and new demands.

But always the seasons change, and this season ushers in the callings of school, work, obligation, and discipline. All the things I try to avoid. But if I have learned just one thing from my journey, it is that resisting change only leads to stagnation. So I take on this change as endings turn into beginnings. I am learning to look for the beauty in the in-between places—circumstantial beauty that needs tremendous patience to mature and bloom. And I know that summer will come again.

I have my future, our futures to consider. And I have today. Today to take care of my girls the best I can. I will take this episode of my life as a sign. I don't have to like it.

In fact, I admit that it sucks. I have a serious aversion to suffering and struggle. But I try to practice acceptance. It is probably one of my biggest challenges.

I also am working on cultivating self-discipline. The discipline to set and accomplish important goals for me and my girls.

Today I feel hopeful. I am doing the best I can and trying not to be so hard on myself as I climb to higher ground. The challenges I face are my cross to bear. That's not to say I deserve this fate or that it is fair. God knows my girls don't deserve this.

But playing the martyr has no appeal. I have a new life to begin. Selling our family home is imminent. Divorce, a likely probability. Moving out West, a certainty. I pray I can handle the challenges set before me, and with the grace of God, I will.

It is undeniably time to move on. Start anew. I am learning what strength, fortitude, and authenticity really mean. I am learning how to live with a broken heart. I am learning how to properly care for myself, alone. I am slowly getting better at asking for and graciously receiving help. I am learning about healing and my own truth. I have been humbled, stripped down.

I regularly stumble on the road of single parenthood and frequently fall while navigating the increasingly rocky path of my girls' adolescence. As I try to make sense of my life and figure out what's next, I am filled with questions. Is it Colorado? Is it freedom from dependency? Is it forgiveness? I long for serenity.

I recommit to self-love, patience, and acting with kindness. I strive to resist comfortable habits that no longer serve. The truth is I don't really know how to make things good again. I am taking tiny steps as I begin to figure out a new life, a new today, and a new tomorrow for me and my girls.

Every ounce of progress takes willpower. But I refuse to let fear lead the way. My girls are my inspiration. My dreams are my motivation. When my mind is quiet, I can see through the chaos to the healthy future we are creating. I breathe deeply and know in my heart that everything will be okay.

About the Author

Jennifer Burman resides in a suburb of Philadelphia with her teenage daughters Eliza and Ava and their dog Dasher. Jennifer spends much of her time wondering about the future and trying to raise her girls to become responsible, well-adjusted women.

A Widow's Walk is her first book. She currently is working on the next one, and she is curious to discover how it will turn out.

Made in the USA
Middletown, DE
28 July 2024

58002761R00124